NO FAR SHORE

in memory of
Mary Fyfe née Reilly (1924-1999)
& Mary Reilly née McNeill (1895-1931)

NO FAR SHORE

Charting Unknown Waters

Anne-Marie Fyfe

Seren is the book imprint of
Poetry Wales Press Ltd,
57 Nolton Street, Bridgend, Wales, CF31 3AE

www.serenbooks.com
facebook.com / SerenBooks
Twitter: @SerenBooks

ISBN: 9781781725177

The publisher acknowledges the financial assistance of the Welsh
Books Council.

Front cover image: Grant Glendinning, www.photoscotland.net

Printed by Ashford Colour Press, Gosport

CONTENTS

1: A First Step

A journey of a thousand miles begins with a single step.
  – Laozi, *Tao Te Ching*

STARTING OUT

In reality the journey begins much earlier, not with that first single step, but with a desire to be somewhere, elsewhere, a destination, and very often, of course, to notice, to observe, to experience the journey itself.

My coastal journey, my charting of the unknown, which begins at my very beginnings and which lacks a known destination, resembles rather a chain of sea's-edge locations on either side of the North Atlantic and originates in a deep desire to be on the coast, to be *back* on the coast, a coast, any coast.

Because 'the coast' is where I started out, took my first steps. And while not all coasts are the same, all coastal locations share the same wonder, the same fear of living on the edge of the depths, the same possibility of stepping out from *terra firma*. All share the promise of that rush of joy as a boat rides out on the waves, share the sudden trepidation as gales and rising tides threaten the breakwater or the sea-wall, share the contemplation of what lies on the far shore, what lies beyond the horizon.

Not that there's anything special about having been born in a coastal town when you come from a country such as Ireland, only 301 miles top-to-bottom, yet with 3,000 miles of coastline and with no point being more than 50 miles from the sea.

In Homer's *Odyssey* the hero is told to take an oar from his *well-found ships* and carry it inland until he finds people

who've never seen an oar. Inlanders, in fact, think it a winnow-
ing fan for separating wheat from chaff, rather than what it is
in the story: a way of separating those who've been to the coast
from those who haven't.

POLES OF INACCESSIBILITY

And while I'm not expecting to encounter too many absolute
inlanders on this voyage around bays, harbours, promonto-
ries, tidal reaches and offshore islands, I do occasionally meet
North Americans who have never been to the ocean, and that's
not just South Dakotans who live 1,000 miles from any coast.
Though even they are closer to the tang of sea-water than
those living on Kazakhstan's borders (at 46.28°N 86.67°E),
1,650 miles from the nearest shoreline, in the most landlocked
place in the world.

I've met their exact opposite too: on isolated Inis Meáin
(53.08°N 9.58°W) off the County Clare coast, where I'd gone,
obviously, for its unworldliness. I talked to an old fisherman
at his front gate one evening, an octogenarian, who'd only
been to the mainland once in all his years, on a day-trip to
Galway: a counterpoint to inlanders who never make it to the
ocean. But, he said, he'd been able to watch every shift and
turn, every flick and shimmer, all the calm and roaring power
of the great Atlantic every single day of his life. A man who'd
charted every water he'd ever need to know.

WAVESOUNDS

My own experience, neither sea-girt nor landlocked, is that of
being born to the call of waves on rocks outside our door, in
the third-last house on Limerick Point (55.08°N 6.06°W) at the
bottom of Dalriada, the shore area in Cushendall, a sea's-edge
first home that my parents had been delighted to find, both
inlanders, both from nine miles farther up in the Glens.

And then a childhood spent around slipway and rockpools,

summer and winter, listening to talk of lobsters and salmon fishing; being lulled to sleep by the tale of the legendary Sea of Moyle below our house and of the mythical swan-children who wintered there for centuries.

Then teenage *Dock of the Bay* years of messing about in boats; years of watching the Scottish coast 14 miles away, across occasionally placid, frequently wild, waters, and, when mist allowed, catching sight of highlands and islands far beyond. And an adult lifetime of crossing and re-crossing that North Channel, between Stranraer on the Galloway coast and Larne in County Antrim, to visit home once I had moved away, and to bring my own children, each year, to share in the summer wonder and the winter vigour of that coastal life.

SEA-FEVER

Naturally the storybooks I loved best, the mobile-library books I borrowed most, took me out to sea, to desert islands and shipwrecks, or to lighthouses, coves and caves, graduating inevitably to Joseph Conrad's charting of the South China Seas and Virginia Woolf's mapping of the deeper channels of the psyche, though never quite shaking off the stark mystery of Wilfrid Gibson's *Flannan Isle*.

More recently I've begun to realise how seriously seawater has seeped into, flooded into, so much of my own writing: the sea, its people – harbourmasters, coastguards, lighthouse keepers, deep-sea captains and their wives and children – and its history of capsizings, drownings, shipwrecks and coastal erosion.

I've been surprised, too, at how often life as a poet has brought me back, not just to my own coast but to coastal towns everywhere, sometimes simply travelling for travel's sake, sometimes researching writers who grew up by, or chose to live by, the sea, or more often now, giving creative-writing workshops and poetry readings in coastal locations – all accompanied by the full orchestra of sound effects, of seawater lapping, or crashing, on the far side of a shingle beach or breakwater, or just beyond a salt-crusted bay window: always invoking the imminent prospect of a launching out from the familiar into the unknown depths.

Like the coastal waters it sets out to explore, this book takes no settled form. It hovers on edges, on shifting shorelines. It weaves a course between prose and poetry. It dips in and out of both, steps continually off the dry land of travel writing, diary and observation. Steps from time to time into a running current, an undersea, of recollection, association and connection. Of objective fact and subjective vision, paragraph by paragraph, fragment by fragment, negotiating an uncharted coastline, as it were, of unpredictable boundaries and, as is always the case with poetry, continually changing margins.

EXULTATION

New England poet Emily Dickinson tells us: *Exultation is the going / Of an inland soul to sea.* Emily was indeed a far-inland soul – I've driven, one long afternoon, the 100 or so miles inland from Boston (42.36°N 71.06°W) to her home in Amherst, an all-day stagecoach journey in Emily's time – but she knew the romance of salt in the air, just as my mother had first tasted it, convalescing from illness as a teenager, in Cushendun, the bay next to Cushendall, all of nine miles from her inland Glenravel home, a bay rich with the sea-air's restorative power.

I like to think of my mother sharing Emily's *exultation* yet again, when, years later, she and my father moved into their house-by-the-sea on Cushendall's Limerick Point, however storm-tossed those first sea's-edge winters would subsequently prove.

And now – to set out in search of that exultation.

2: Journeying Mapless

If this book of mine fails to take a straight course,
it is because I am lost in a strange region: I have no map.
— Graham Greene, *The End of the Affair*

MAPLESS IN MONROVIA

Seriously? Journeying without maps?

Ancient wisdom would have us believe that it's better to travel expectantly than to arrive. But getting to a destination is definitely still on most of our agendas.

Graham Greene was perhaps so taken with his literal and uncharted *Journey Without Maps*, to Liberia in 1936, that he went on to use the concept figuratively in the opening of his novel *The End of the Affair*. But *the heart of the matter* is that matters of the heart, of the emotions, are invariably a journey without maps.

Greene would have little excuse now for being mapless in Monrovia, or anywhere else. Years back, after much long-distance driving through Eastern Europe, I planned a road-trek all the way to Moscow, only to be confronted (in the latter pages of the large-scale *European Roadmap* on which I'd long relied) with vast white expanses beyond Romania: not a mapmaker's impression of snow-covered *versts*, clearly not uncharted lands, but simply a lack, before *the Wall came down*, of sufficient access to shared data on our side of the Danube or the Dniester. That's all solved now, though, and there's an extra SatNav disk I could buy that would take me to St. Petersburg, or Murmansk, or even Vladivostok.

AN ENCHANTMENT OF MAPS

Crumpled on the Hillman Hunter's passenger seat,
pinned on St Mary's Primary 7 side wall,
maybe the classroom globe spinning,
the flip-out gazetteer in the back-fold of a diary
(embossed *Fyfes Motors* or *Firestone*),
a threadbare-by-O-Level Philip's atlas,
two travel-bleached OS quarter-inch-series
dark in a tallboy drawer,
all promising passage to the well-thumbed, dog-eared
reality beyond our Dalriada Avenue,
all mere two-dimensional intimations
of illimitable possible worlds.

Tinny axis-rattling revolutions
of a Christmas-morning globe: I am eight,
finger-tracing shivers of Alaska,
Bolivia, Canberra,
tracking latitudes, Tropics-of-, peninsulas,
Abyssinia & Dar-es-Salaam
outdoing the others with the plangent music
of the *Thousand & One Nights*.

NO READABLE MAP

End of each annual fortnight & North-West Donegal
will have another yellowing Sellotaped rip on a fold
(a fold that could matter one day)
between two towns & a lost river,
thread separating from glued binding,
from folding & refolding
our compacted paper kingdoms
back-to-front & inside-out.

The map-stack in the Hillman's glove-compartment
(*glove*-compartment? when has *that* locked box
ever seen motoring gauntlets,

Fair-Isle mittens, Sunday kid-gloves?),
a trove that includes the gift of a Michelin *España*
we have no plans to use,
no language to access.
An accreting, expanding, treasure-chest,
verging on the unshuttable,
a veritable chartroom locker,
reluctantly sharing its cramped map-space with:

> stray Glacier mints, no bag,
> a *Pope John the Twenty-Third* Sunday missal,
> a Junior Mole wrench,
> a blunt Revlon lipstick – *Cherries in the Snow*,
> a praying plastic Blessed Virgin of Lourdes water
> replenished after each Easter Vigil.

BLOOD TIES

My brothers vie for back-seat possession
of the mail-order 'motorist' compass,
bicker over which way the spread-out map
should lie across their bony knees.

The needle bobs reckless
on most of our routes,
shudders helpless
on the Seven Mile Straight's nauseating switchback.

> Index-fingers trace ripple-red veins,
> B-roads & the unmarked.
> (The unmarked…which roads
> would remain unmarked? Which of *us*?)

We *um* & *ah* over customs posts, ancient monuments,
a bridge, what the map calls an 'R.C. Church',

> squabble over the complex
> business of these vital charts,

over the exactitude of their longitudes,
the exactings of longing,
the abyss of a no-map's-land.

AND THEN THE RAINS CAME

In the deluge of a Portnoo August fortnight,
days of *ennui* pending a cessation,
confined to a cliff-house parlour
at a picture window that could easily be
high out on an Atlantic swell (full sound FX…),
we're told off for vandalising last year's
AA Guide-to-Ireland's back pages.

All those damp hours of cutting, folding,
metamorphosing into a flotilla of paper sailboats,
perfectly pleated,
mine a *Girona*, Gerard's
would have to be – of course,
from his illustrated *Look & Learns* –
the Duke of Medina Sidonia's flagship
far from a known shore
& foundering on the local rocks.

Wet days & we're totally off-scale.
My father cites more & more unreachable
destinations, on no map whatsoever,
destinations we'll be setting out for
any minute now – *definitely*
– *any minute now – just as soon as that rain lifts.*

Setting out, perhaps, for the heart
of a mapless Africa, maybe even
to Timbuktu, my father's ultimate rainy-day threat.

OBSESSION

Could it be that I'm obsessed, then, with these cryptic two-dimensional representations of the three-dimensional world? With being able to see, and fold away, reality?

Of course, as a writer, I'm already obsessed with putting the world down on paper, with mapping in print the details of the journey, whether landscape or life-scape, but most of us, as writers, have *put aside the childish thing* of needing to see a picture of where we're going, of needing to know *are we nearly there yet*, just as most of us, as drivers, have abandoned the business of unfolding, and shuffling, and peering at, printed maps, in some dimly-lit roadside spot, relying now on the trustworthy, authoritative tones of our SatNavs and GPSs.

But didn't the storytellers who delighted us most as children and teenagers always include a map in the endpapers? Like Robert Louis Stevenson's ornate and detailed realisation of *Treasure Island*'s hills, woods and offshore depths, that mapped reward and danger in equal measure.

DEAD MAN'S CHEST

The quest (where there's a quest there's a chart)
is always to lay claim
to Flint's buried Spanish gold.

My Woolworths sketchbooks have countless
repeated X-marks-the-spot outlines in red,
with their own complex system of grids,
secret espionage codes in alternating
lower & upper case,
all finely traced out in reverse.

I highlight the pitfalls,
severed rope-bridges,
an overshot pine forest,

collapsed river-banks.
I establish positions,
botanically exact symbols
for previously unclassified species,
plan to head North by North-North-West,
that's what the Gazetteer advises.

Oh, & I remember to pack a rucksack with tomatoes,
Dairylea Triangles & buttered Veda.

CAPTAIN FLINT'S SIGNATURE

Point Lobos (36.52°N 121.94°W), just below Carmel in Califor-
nia and the model for *Treasure Island*, is not an actual island,
but from where Robert Louis Stevenson lived on the opposite
peninsula it sure looks just like one: and every cove I've visited
around the Point echoes a detail of the story. Although creating
a fictional map is, according to Stevenson, far from straight-
forward.

> It is one thing to draw a map at random...It is quite
> another to have to examine a whole book, make an
> inventory of all the allusions contained in it, and
> with a pair of compasses, painfully design a map to
> suit the data. I did it; and the map was drawn again
> in my father's office, with embellishments of blow-
> ing whales and sailing ships, and my father himself
> brought into service a knack he had of various writ-
> ing, and elaborately FORGED the signature of
> Captain Flint, and the sailing directions of Billy
> Bones.

How strange that would have seemed to us as children, Robert
Louis Stevenson matching image to story, checking 'continu-
ity'. Stranger still, those respectable and diligent Scottish
draughtsmen of the Stevenson lighthouse company using
their cartographic skills to illustrate a children's story for the
Chief Engineer's son.

17

MARKING THE SPOT

Retrieving lost treasure is never simply a children's game, though. American poet Elizabeth Bishop buried her mother's brooch in the garden of her maternal grandparents' Great Village home, on Nova Scotia's Cobequid Bay. Years later, long after her mother had been taken to Dartmouth Asylum, Bishop was unable to reclaim that one token, simply because she hadn't drawn a map.

Yes, during a stay in that happy/sad house on my journey, I was obviously tempted to search every inch of the garden, but to what depth? (Surely Elizabeth would, over the many years in which she returned there, have had that very same thought?)

And to what end? I have my own places to find on this journey. Perhaps we don't make a map of our lives at the time, as it doesn't occur to us that we'll ever need to find our way back there. Perhaps 'back' isn't where we ever want to go.

3: Oceans of Truth

...like a boy playing on the sea-shore and diverting myself
now and then finding a smoother pebble
or a prettier shell than ordinary,
whilst the great ocean of truth lay all undiscovered before me.
– Isaac Newton

UNCHARTED WATERS

So I need coastal and island maps, and maps of the roads that will take me there, though not all the territories I'm about to explore will yield, I know, to the simple discipline of road-naming.

Walking recently on Achill, Ireland's largest island (54°N 10°W), off County Mayo, I found most verbal directions involved taking 'the sea road': every road, one way or another, leading, it seemed, back to the surrounding sea.

Perhaps it wasn't a lack of maps that struck Graham Greene on Achill during the non-fictional love affair for whose fictional end his first-person narrator had, it seems, *no map* (in the epigraph to 2: *Journeying Mapless*). With so many different roads on Achill referred to simply as 'the sea road', any attempt at mapping his island of dreams, his escape from reality, would have seemed quixotically impractical.

Perhaps it won't be so easy to find the road to the sea's edge, at the end of which – at the beginning of my family story – a young couple close the door on the outside world.

THE SEA ROAD

A groom & bride walking
hand in hand the Sea Road's length
to a stark last house by the point.
East-facing windows shuttered
tight on the other two houses.
                              I greet
the newly married pair with the usual
nothings, but they pass unseeing.

I stop at the brow of the hill
& look back to the shore,
to a tiny weather-house couple
pulling closed
                    an ocean-blue front door.
Shut tight against the sea-air of melancholy
that hangs over all these sea roads.

STANDING AT STANFORDS

If they were to be found anywhere, the maps of coasts and
islands and inlets I have in mind for this quest, it would surely
be at Stanfords in London's Long Acre, reputedly the busiest
cartographers in the world. But *the science of cartography*, Irish
poet Eavan Boland insists in one of her poem-titles, *is limited*:
while *the cartographer,* in one of Jamaican Kei Miller's poems,
tries unsuccessfully *to map a way to Zion.*

Maybe both writers had already visited Stanfords, with its
Aladdin's cave of maps, its whole world of maps, and found
that the places they sought – does everyone have a quest? –
were uncharted waters. Perhaps even Joseph Conrad's world-
weary narrator, Marlow, when he stood staring into the future
(*The horror!*) outside Stanfords' Victorian shop windows,
grasped that the journey he was about to take into the *Heart of
Darkness* would be undertaken unaided, into uncharted terri-
tories.

TRUTHS ABOUT HOME

Perhaps cartography's purest gift to us
is the exact, the definitive,
land-sea interface line,
where green/brown contours meet the blues: pale blue,
medium, dark, wine-dark-dark, midnight blue,
but all of them sea-blues.

Home
– or the nearest I can pinpoint
to the meaning of home on any map –
is right on the pencil-thin tideline
on the very sea's-edge of that interface.

WALL MAPS AND CHARTROOMS

I've always had maps on one or another wall wherever I've
lived. The Europe map, on my teenage son's bedroom wall,
that the whole family consulted. Then a map of the Santa Cate-
rina area of Brazil when my daughter lived there on a gap year.
And now a study-wall chart, tracking with multicoloured
push pins my recent years' world travel.

But how could one piece together – that's the question – a
coherent map of this strange coastal itinerary that's taking me
round Wales, England's East and South-West coasts and the
Scottish Highlands and Islands, as well as from Antrim to
Cork and back, and on to Massachusetts, Maine, New
Brunswick and Nova Scotia? Taking me back particularly to
the Western Isles my Scots forebears left years ago, sailing for
Antrim's rugged coast and glens?

Of course it's land-maps, road-maps, that I'd want, not sea-
charts, which would be a mystery to me anyway, though the
image of a weathered sea captain in the chartroom, elbows on
a spread scroll, with rulers, dividers, sextant and marine
chronometer to hand, still brims with excitement, with poten-
tial, whether it's of Captain Smith on the fated *Titanic*, or Vasco

da Gama from 500 years earlier, watching us from Master McAuley's classroom wall.

I've stood in awe in the heavily waxed boardroom of the Commissioners of Northern Lights, at their grandly Georgian HQ on Edinburgh's George Street, where august Presbyterian gentlemen commissioned various Stevensons (including Thomas, Robert Louis's father, of the forged Captain Flint autograph), and I've gazed there at a vast map of the many lighthouses in the Commissioners' charge. But it's still essentially a land map. Even far out at sea, beyond that pencil-thin line, lighthouses are part of our landside domain, reminders of fear of the deep.

MAPPING THE UNMAPPABLE

In which maps are just one way of describing a voyage

in which worlds are only part geography,
part tales of love & detachment.
Early years are both land & sea-deep.
Early is idyllic,
high grasses & year-round sea-clover,
a cluster of brightly lit
Christmas-tree days
above a winter sea
at the year's stormy end.

The year I turn eleven
my young father suffers a stroke.
Though he quickly regains strength,
he then watches my mother,
suddenly fearful of an ebbing future,
& drawn to a distant place
with no trail of white beach-stones to lead her back.

The year that, as a family,
we step over the deep's pencil-line,

far out from dry land,
no charts to show us sea routes home,
home to the known, the familiar:

stepping ashore just once would be a godsend.

COMING HOME LATE

But I'm setting out now, late as it is,
on that long voyage home,
back to that land or wherever,
tracing misfortunes, uncertainty,
a family hiatus, yearlong absences:

I'm blanking out the controlling GPS voice,
selecting every wrong turn if I so wish,
guessing by now at what's hidden
in the worn Sellotaped folds.

The territory is coastlines,
islands, the liminal,
headlands that reach out to the far deep,
down to the fathomed, unfathomable sea floor.

PACKING MY BAGS

The truth is that my quest for some sort of edge-of-the-depths
understanding has to be a coastwise journey without maps.
But not without guides: Herman Melville, Emily Dickinson,
Joseph Conrad, Elizabeth Bishop, Robert Louis Stevenson,
Virginia Woolf and many more, all in my traveller's kitbag.

4: Always on Edges

> *La mer, la mer, toujours recommencée!*
> – Paul Valéry, *Le cimitière marin*

SHORELINE

The high sea-wall, a beach-hut's paint blister,
four cormorants, oars & floats,
the sadness of a deflated beach ball,

fish-scales clustering like my brother's stamp-hinges,
rock-crusted limpets with slimy insides,

a pinch of sand in salty tomato sandwiches,
buckets without spades, the rubberiness of kelp,

limestone headlands, ex-Navy binoculars,
a pink-petalled bathing cap,
bamboo fishing net, conical shells,
perfect skimming-stones,

our family saloon reversing close to a pier's edge,
a stench of lugworm, July sandcastles
that were always too wet, too dry,

weather closing in, the cancelled Sunday Regatta,
the clarity of Limerick Point rockpools.

TO RE-BEGIN AT THE BEGINNING

A constant recurrence, a re-beginning, every day, month, year,
since I started writing. In fact since I started life. Started play-
ing on the slipway opposite our first front door, with the tide
constantly recurring, a repeated motif.

And days, months, years, of exposure to other coastal places, either side of the Atlantic, haven't eased the longing for those first Sea of Moyle waves, for the slipway, Limerick Point, Dalriada, the cliff path and Salmon Port, the horizon framed to the right by Garron Point and to the left by Layde, the headland that defined our bay's northern edge, and always slipping in and out of a misty reality, the Mull of Kintyre's far shore.

Those years haven't lessened, either, the memory of people I grew up among in Dalriada whose livelihood was the sea, both those who sailed deep-sea or worked coastal vessels and ferries, and those who worked at 'the fishing' locally, men such as John Finlay, John Roy and Danny McIlroy.

One long-term consequence of having Annie Finlay as a neighbour is my failure to regard fresh lobster with the culinary reverence it's usually accorded, seeing it, in season, as daily fare, as it is in lobster shacks all up and down US East and West Coasts.

THE FISHING HUT

John Finlay's 'fishing' was beyond Layde at Cushendun: I might now locate his fishing hut as being across the bay from poet Moira O'Neill's Rockport, the house Louis MacNeice describes in his poem *Cushendun*, written on the eve of war. Or locate it as being by the Mediterranean-white 1930s Bay Café on the path to the caves and to the Crommelin family's eccentrically secluded Cave House, the house that Constance Crommelin's husband, English Poet Laureate, John Masefield, longed for when in London. All three 'Cushendun' poets unable to prevent the sea and its headlands and islands from encroaching and re-encroaching on the written word.

But my interest back then wasn't in famous poetic connections but in the entirely unliterary knowledge that our neighbour, John Finlay, didn't simply go to bed in his house at the regulated hour, but loaded up a van's worth of gear and drove over

Layde to the next bay to sleep in that shore hut until perhaps three or four in the morning before pushing his fishing boat out onto dark bay waters.

With how much seriousness can adults appear to invest the humouring of children's need for adventure? When John Finlay appeared to give in to our pleas for a shore-hut night, he must have known that after the excitement of strong, midnight, Primus-stove tea, and digestive biscuits from a tin, we would quickly find the single-windowed darkness too eerie: though there was time enough for him to get us back to waiting parents in Dalriada, and still drive back to the fishing hut without us, to catch what was left of a short night's sleep.

WRITING ON THE WATER

My first poetry publication was, unsurprisingly, *A House By The Sea*, followed by *Late Crossing* (another sea-reference, or at least North-Channel reference) complete with a poem, *Outboard*, about John Finlay in his final illness.

Late Crossing also has one poem called simply *The Sea of Moyle* in which I ask the question that had whispered throughout my adult years of shuttling between London and Cushendall: *what brings me back here, year after year?* The answer, inevitably, in the poem, is: *I'd say it's the sea every time.*

Even, in my latest, my fifth, collection, I still found myself going back, still found myself writing about slipways and headlands and tides, and about the people among whom I grew up.

I don't ever expect to free myself of the mix of excitement and dread that comes from staring out into the unknowable, the indeterminate, and maybe that's a significant metaphor in my life. Which is why I decided to confront whatever it is that has some of us constantly looking out to islands, or far horizons, and wondering.

ON THE SLIPWAY

A gutting-knife's moon-glistened blade,
cable-stitch of John Roy's nubbly gansey,
the shudder on first looking at a dogfish,

eerily giant footprints in wet sand,
cooling slap of calamine lotion after sunshine,
my uncle's accordion shanties from a darkening porch,

dip & pull of each oar in serious waters, the stark white
of our house from this side of the point,
that homecoming judder
as a keel grates on beach stones once again.

WAVES OF POETRY CRASHING THE SEA-WALL

So, what was it actually like, growing up on the edge of something vast and exciting, on the edge of both calm and danger?

Wildness was surely there in poetry written about the Antrim Coast and it was pretty clear, from stories we heard in childhood, that being doomed to live by our Sea of Moyle, whose cold waves crashed night and day on the volcanic rocks below our house, was the cruellest punishment a wicked stepmother could conjure up, for Fionnuala and her brothers Aodh, Fiachra and Conn, in the legend of *The Children of Lír*.

When you're only six years old a 300-year 'sentence' seems more than eternity.

Though the punishment of turning the children into swans actually seemed somehow beautifully poetic, almost balletic, in contrast to the choppy, rough November waves I watched from my bedroom window.

And yet we weren't alone in our myths: reading Ovid's *Metamorphoses* I found (and appropriated for my contribution to a poetry anthology entitled *Metamorphic*) the Greek tale of another daughter turned into a bird as punishment. Surely the Scylla in that story must be the heron from my first poems, wintering on the rocky shore below Metson's field, awaiting, it would appear, the return of Fionnuala and her swan siblings?

NOW RETURNED HOME

Few longed for the heady sea's-edge mix of excitement and dread quite as hungrily as Californian poet, Robinson Jeffers, who, in the late 1920s, lived with his wife Una and their children in a cottage outside Knocknacarry, behind Layde headland and between Cushendun's and Cushendall's bays. The Jefferses, at home, already looked out from the wildest imaginable edge, a remote, rocky outcrop on America's West Coast, between Monterey Peninsula and Big Sur (overlooking Robert Louis Stevenson's Point Lobos): but the poet in Robinson Jeffers aspired to something even wilder, even more remote, and chose the Antrim coast.

And yet not so strange, perhaps, to find American writers fascinated by our coastline, as its landscape and legends were widely known through both Lady Gregory's and Thomas Moore's versions of *The Children of Lír* and through Moira O'Neill's early 20th-century poetry. Exiled in Canada, O'Neill re-imagined the Antrim Coast, Rathlin, and Garron Point in poems recognised in their day both by Charles Villiers Stanford's setting them to music and by their inclusion in WB Yeats's 1895 *Book of Irish Verse*.

QUICK-TEMPERED

In *At Shane O'Neill's Cairn* Robinson Jeffers describes *the gray waters of the Moyle,* and in another Glens poem, *Ossian's Grave,* we find him gazing out *Toward Scotland, and the quick-tempered Moyle.* The perfect epithet, as the mercurial scene, whether seen from Jeffers's perspective or from my bedroom window,

29

altered with every change in weather, whole far shores disappearing: misty mountains of Scotland's highlands and islands looming imperious one moment, the next apparently submerged, Atlantis-like.

Even the nearest point-of-reference, majestic Garron Point, at the southern end of our bay, shifted continually from sunlit basking to sudden louring, to complete disappearance in yet another squally shower, another sea mist rolling in. The Jefferses made Knocknacarry their base for touring all of Ireland, much of Scotland and a little of England (including meeting in London with Leonard and Virginia Woolf), as it was the Antrim coast that had enthralled them. Robinson wrote to a friend saying that, if he didn't already live on the Californian coast, the one place in the world he would choose to live would be on top of Fair Head, a 600-foot precipice between Cushendun and Ballycastle, that looks out over Rathlin Island. Yet much as he dramatised our rugged coastline, his sad and moving poem *Now Returned Home* (on sailing to Barra in the Western Isles) does recognise the harsh, sometimes heartbreaking, realities behind his idealised starkness and isolation.

LA BOCCA DEL DIAVOLO

Growing up in Dalriada we always had dogs at home, collies and later a labrador, and dogs are born swimmers. At least ours had to be, as our playing-on-the-rocks ritual involved throwing Moss or Dandy off the rocks and watching the dog work her way back to where she could actually clamber up out of the surf – which meant her doggy-paddling the whole way back round to the slipway.

The launch point was always *The Devil's Mouth* – imagine the churned up infernal stretch of water which gave rise to that name, the stretch I always saw when we were told of Jesus's storm-tossed walking-on-water.

What's shocking isn't merely the surprise North Channel temperatures must have been for the dog, but the fact that, aged seven or eight, I was throwing a full size collie off those rocks and I'm amazed now the force didn't suddenly take me into the waves along with the dog!

Yet I've watched similar swimming-dog scenes repeated in harbours everywhere – Dooega on Achill, Castlebay on Barra, Mackerel Cove on Maine's Bailey Island, as dog-owners show off their glossy hounds' swimming prowess and their own ability to pitch a tennis ball quite so far out, forgetting that we can all find ourselves suddenly, unexpectedly, out of our depths.

THE HARBOUR

There's always a dog swimming towards the slipway.
Sleek-headed, otterlike, bobbing,
a dog that never reaches land.

> You can wade out on the stone beds, with the dog
> always approaching, closing on you. You can call,
>   *I'm coming. Hold on, I'm coming,*
> but the dog will have vanished, for sure.

>   All day you'll stay perplexed
>   by that vision of sea-surface,
>   the silent movie of the dog's last frames,
>   edging near, tantalisingly near.

Leaving harbour, returning, leaving, returning.

That last hundred yards
between redemption & reproach.

> *Did the dog bark?*, they'll ask after. And, *Yes*, you'll say
>   *I'm sure he barked. I'm certain he wanted to be saved.*

Should I have been worried I can't swim? Can't even
doggy-paddle?

Barking, barking, loudly, louder.
The sea wins every time.

How many people are in the water?
How many dogs are swimming safely to shore?
How long can any of us hold this breath?

5: Tidelines

TIDAL, RISING

One looks for storms at the spring equinox –
yet it is the September equinox that drowns.
— Helen Waddell, *Peter Abelard*

The very essence of nothingness.

Tides are alive to the tiniest scythe of moonlight,
still yearn to see the world slant on a true horizon.

Yesterday's much-heralded high tide arrived
with something less than a whimper: by daylight
we'd lost sight of our seafront's carnival lights.

Tides long for stately white sails to disturb
the Prussian blue with an elaborate grace.

For years they lie low on a seabed sensitive
to the minutest tremor – timely, sly, opportunistic.

Whole streetgangs of tides rattle the front doors
of childhood. Just one day, in April,
then slink away, leave a telltale froth
on the pea-shingle.

A swift retreating ebb is best for early regret,
for reflection.

Never, ever, underestimate
a neap tide's mortal trickery, they say.

While our children sleep on land
the moon gently sucks up our seven seas.

There's a solitary tide behind each & every shipwreck,
a single swell that started out as a shiver
way, way back in another era

& doesn't know its own full-grown strength.

And, oh, how a rogue tide's amplitude
tangles with our wishful seascape.

You can spend a lifetime scanning night's horizons
& never get to see a comet fall far out in the deep.

What was it, I wonder, about the lunar tide,
that I detected in your gaze
the morning you left for the island ferry?

6: Call me Ishmael

LANSINGBURGH, NEW YORK STATE

Moby Dick is an early mobile-library favourite
(Friday afternoons, Bridge Street, Cushendall).

Years later my cousin, Mary Ellen
(her grandmother, my Great-Aunt Rose,
shipped out of Belfast's Clarendon Dock
Montreal-bound in 1911),
lives in the Melville family house,
far from our grey Friday library van.
From Herman's study we watch
a broad gushy Hudson in snow & slush,
rush its own long-mapped route
down to wide & treacherous ocean-charts.

We might even wonder what that Ishmaelite meant by:
It is not down on any map. True places never are!

> Those are the true places I hope to find.
> And map. To prove him wrong.
> That voyager out of Nantucket.

Maybe, just maybe, the true places can be mapped:
even the very deep ones.

TRUE PLACES

Chart-doubting Melville hadn't actually been to Nantucket
when he challenged his *Moby Dick* readers: *Nantucket! Take out
your map and look at it. See what a real corner of the world it occupies.*
Just nineteen years old when he first left his Lansingburgh

home at the north-most reach of the Hudson's tidal waters (42.78°N 73.66°W) and made for the Atlantic's far side, signing up on a Liverpool-bound merchant ship, Herman would be thirty-three before he visited the coastal island on which he'd based *Moby Dick*, its name adapted from Algonquin words meaning, it's thought, 'faraway island'.

It was the year *after* his epic was published, and he would find that places could exist on maps and be true places nonetheless. As I find, taking the Nantucket (41.28°N 70.10°W) ferry from Cape Cod's Hyannis Harbor on a cold April morning.

Melville picked his fictional crew from around the world (even one from Belfast) but his officers were all from right here, third mate Flask from Tisbury on nearby Martha's Vineyard, second mate Stubb from Cape Cod itself, and first mate, Starbuck, a Nantucketer, and a born whaler, like five of the other crewmen and Captain Ahab himself.

LIME-GREEN MACAROONS

Visiting Nantucket's Whaling Museum is a confrontation on a wholly unexpected scale: leviathan whale skeletons (though none of them quite matching the vastness of Ahab's nemesis), huge, ominous-looking blubber vats, and lighthouse lamps, gigantic bulbs visible 30 miles out *via* their complex louvred lenses.

And, offering a hint of 19th-century refinement on the day I arrived, plates of pink, purple and lime-green macaroons dotted around the exhibits for refreshment. Not regular whalers' hardtack for sure. But Elizabeth Bishop would certainly have appreciated their incongruity: during her Vassar college years she spent a Christmas week with a friend on Nantucket *sipping sherry with the lighthouse keeper's wife*!

An island awash with yellow flowers decorating every shop, café and streetlamp. Nantucket's Daffodil Week. Brant Point

Light is accessed *via* a long and sea-bleached board gangway to the lighthouse door (red-painted boards worn bare in the centre). Lighthouse, too, festooned with *a crowd, a host of…*

And at the beach-head close by, a lone shack, like our old neighbour John Finlay's fishing hut – in which I still want to sleep a few hours on a hard bench and push out in 3am silence across a bay, any bay, to check the nets. Salt-encrusted windows, a rusted padlock, deep in weeds, all the old magic still there, still here.

7: Beyond That Horizon

Beyond the horizon, across the divide
'Round about midnight, we'll be on the same side...
– Bob Dylan, *Beyond the Horizon*

BLUE POCKET DICTIONARY

Horizon: (*n.*) line at which the earth's surface & the sky appear to meet
Rowing: (*n.*) sport or pastime of propelling a boat by means of oars
Oar: (*n.*) pole with a flat blade, used to row or steer a boat through water

ON THE EDGE

Perhaps all our trips to the ocean's edge are driven by the need to contemplate what happens at land's outer limits, on far headlands, on the edges of the tide. Or perhaps it is only the horizon that has us hypnotized with the urge to contemplate our one quotidian hint of the infinite.

To the moon and back is as nothing compared to the paradox of unreachability that is the straight stark line which, we know, curves, in reality, both left to right and away from us: so inviting, so always out of our grasp.

TAKE A LINE, A PLUMB LINE:

1. Fact: horizons are ultimately unknowable.
2. Fiction: you can see the horizon.
3. Myth: it is possible to travel beyond the horizon.
4. Proposition: horizons are evidence of a parallel world.

HORIZON GAZING

Who would choose to gaze endlessly on such an enigma? Well, the novelist, Joseph Conrad for one, who said he disliked living anywhere he could not see the horizon. And anyone who grew up with that intangible edge in their sights. Not to mention the hundreds and thousands who travel weekly, seasonally, to the sea's edge to be transfixed equally by its visible and invisible presences.

We always tell ourselves there's nothing out there, just the odd tiny ship passing, but maybe we're deluded. Would all our ambitions, desires, longings be fulfilled if we could simply cross that line?

Elizabeth Bishop once tellingly described the horizon as being boat-shaped. Should we then take a small boat and make the attempt, perhaps find Utopia?

LIMITATIONS, SEEING CLEARLY

> *Warning*: objects on the horizon
> may be closer than they appear.

STAKING A CLAIM

I've never met a single soul who's been to the horizon
& returned to tell the tale. And there's nowhere
on a floating edge to plant a flag
(like you'd do on a moon-crater).
So who'd ever believe you?

VISIBILITY / LOST HORIZONS

> *Row, row, row your boat*
> you sang, once.
> Gently, merrily, gently.
> Like all straight lines, this horizon *is but a dream.*

LEXICON

Row, rowing, rowed, to row,
variations you checked, aged eight,
in a blue pocket dictionary (Concise Oxford)
bought in Stewart McElheran, Stationers, Ballymena,
long before you were a schoolgirl in that town.

VANISHING POINT

Earlier today my horizons disappeared.
No trace of lines between sky & sea.
No joins, no delineations, between earth & the heavens.
I steady my gaze on a point
where the line ought to be.
Dizzy with silvering possibilities.

OARS

Back to those misapprehended winnows:
choose carefully, the chandler's
awaiting your call.
Ash, Cherry, Walnut, Maple?

DISORIENTATION

It's a foolhardy man who loses sight of the horizon.

ALBATROSS

You're on the verge, don't look at the drop ahead,
keep your eye on that high ten-foot wingspan.
Is it true, as explorers once believed,
you could sail clean off the edge?

A BACKWARD GLANCE

Old sea-dogs leaving port will say,
if you look round the voyage is fated.

When is it ever safe to turn?
OK, let's just keep that horizon squarely in our sights.

A GLASS DARKLY

Does prayer help? Emily D,
our shipboard philosopher, would have us
praying Horizons, focusing at eye-level
in order to ascend on high. Emily, at home,
our most intrepid voyager into the unknown.

EXITS & ENTRANCES

All the horizon's a stage.
Always someone walking from wings,
taking downstage centre,
leaving those of us in the front row
blindsided, awed, afraid.

SCOPE/INFINITE

Those plastic ships you fished
out of Cornflakes boxes from McAlister's
still inch along dormant synapses,
still skirt the rising horizon of wakefulness.
Always intended to tantalise.

ITHACA

Pull against the expected gales. Occasionally
you'll have the comfort
of a following wind. Mostly
the effort will tax your strength,
tap every reserve. Westerlies
have no love for sailors, are
indifferent to your destination.

FLATLINING

You mustn't sleep. Think about Amelia Earhart's lone round-the-world flights. How she fought, gave in for seconds, maybe minutes, & then the shock of the moment when she'd find herself fully awake again. All pilots fear the degree bank, the lost horizon.

MINDSCAPE

Toughest jigsaw
I attempted as a child
had a serrated horizon.
Clouds obscured the line.
You couldn't tell if there were pieces
missing. The bigger picture is the zigzagging,
made up as you go along.

CURVEBALL

Don't ever trust an empty horizon.
Even the painted cardboard cut-out ships
crossing in slow motion are there to deceive,
only there to lure you into the deeps.

EXALTATION

When did God divide the waters?, we were asked at Primary School. *And in which day of creation? Was it all one great ocean?* In Geography we'd list sea names. Sargasso was the favourite. Then oceans, Pacific always first. Columns filled our exercise books. *Just when in the seven days did the horizon emerge between earth & the firmament?*

OUTER LIMITS

When you reach the horizon
rest oars, check watch,

to the second, complete the log.
Lean back, look out to sea.
Is that the horizon of home?
A straight empty line like this.
To which you can never return.

8: Chasing Sandpipers

> *The roaring alongside he takes for granted,*
> *and that every so often the world is bound to shake.*
> *He runs, he runs to the south...*
> – Elizabeth Bishop, *The Sandpiper*

A VOYAGE?

Hugging coastlines, indented, complicated and perverse as they are, with or without maps, even crossing by bridge, ferry and causeway to a hundred islands, doesn't constitute a 'voyage' (something few undertake nowadays anyway). Even a sea-journey isn't automatically a Conradian or a Coleridgean 'voyage'. And yet I felt that stepping off dry land and journeying into my own past was a tantalising, an essential, voyage.

A voyage whose sailing orders included not simply visiting inshore waters round Suffolk, Devon, Cornish and Welsh shorelines, as well as Caithness and the Moray Firth, but crossings by ferry to Orkney and the Hebrides, to Antrim, Cork and Wexford. And then, on the Atlantic's far side, exploring America's north-eastern seaboard, right up to Prince Edward Island and Nova Scotia in Canada's Maritime Provinces. Looking for how coastal folk live on the edge of the known, and for how they cope with not knowing what the seas will do next, with the unknown lying beneath deceptively calm surfaces.

What drew me to Nova Scotia in particular? Weren't the great seaport of Boston, the whaling island of Nantucket, the elites' escape at Martha's Vineyard and the lighthouses of Cape Cod, discovery enough? Part of the desire to go farther was Elizabeth Bishop, whom I'd always thought of as a Massachusetts poet, but whom I've gradually come to recognise as 'the' poet of the Canadian Maritimes.

I'd always admired Bishop's writing about coastlines, islands and geography: and although she lived in Brazil later in life, she spent her early years in her maternal grandparents' home in a Nova Scotia community simply called Great Village (45.41°N 63.60°W), which I'd always imagined would be very like my own home village on the Antrim coast. As it proved, with its school, two churches, post office, volunteer fire brigade and two filling stations, one of which belonged to Bishop's uncle. The other, the ESSO station opposite her grandmother's house (that gave her the $ESSO-SO-SO-SO$ line in her filling-station poem), took me right back to my own grandmother's farm in Glenravel, with its lone ESSO pump on the main road at the end of the lane.

I've gradually come to see more significance in Bishop's Bulmer (maternal) Nova Scotia background than in her Bishop (paternal) Boston upbringing: unsurprising, perhaps, as her father died within months of her birth. And I've become increasingly interested in the impact, on her life and writing, of the absence of both parents but especially of her mother in crucial childhood years.

INSCRUTABLE HOUSES

So visiting Great Village (and discovering just how alike our small coastal towns actually were) was to become part of that exploration. Being invited to spend time in the house in which Bishop spent those childhood years gave me a precious opportunity to reflect on the child who, as her grandmother sings, in Bishop's poem *Sestina*, draws one after another *inscrutable house*, a child I'd already encountered in one of my own first poems in which my mother talks of the loss of her parents and I recall that *I stopped drawing perfect houses for perfect families even before my mother got sick.*

And to sleep in the house was an even more compelling experience, including the chance to observe the Nova Scotia night through Bishop's bedroom skylight. She describes, in an unpublished autobiographical novel, one of many treasures on bookshelves there, how the sky *pressed down and dull on the dark skylight*; how half-asleep, half awake, she imagined the sky gathering to raindrops that *plop, seemed to flatten themselves against the icy glass like snubbed noses or splashed out bullets. And I'd stare back till my eyes ran tears.*

It was a unique engagement with a writer's deep past, but one tinged continually over those days with unease, as I realised that missing mothers, Elizabeth Bishop's, mine, my mother's and more, were becoming a persistent theme on my quest.

SEA-FRONT HOUSE

She's framed again in the doorway
of our old sea-front home,
arms outstretched, palms upwards,
wearing a plaid skirt, a pale
lemon sweater,
& behind her there's still the wreckage.

Way out on the sky's edge
two sets of trawler lights converge
at 4.20am,
an hour when the body's
resistance is at its lowest.

Do we really eyeflick 2000
times per minute?

O Holy Night
sounds through the *weary world*
& she asks again *Is it still dark out there?*

I walk to the front gate,
another ship's light in the distance,
a neighbour's lamp burns.

The cries of the bereft ring truest
in these hours.

Is there anyone awake in the firmament?

BEING AN ISLAND

It wasn't simply Elizabeth Bishop's hankering after North
American and Brazilian shorelines that captivated me, though,
but the fact that she'd visited our own Antrim coastline on a
1930's motoring tour. I like to think of her stopping for 'gaso-
line' at my grandmother's petrol-pump, then driving down
Glenariffe to Cushendall, down Bridge Street and along Mill
Street, out past the school where, years later, I would spin that
classroom globe round to Canada perhaps, or learn *The Skye
Boat Song*. Then on past the churches, the old courthouse and
the 1930s cinema (established by our next-door Dalriada
neighbour Mrs Wann) and out onto the Antrim Coast Road,
one of so many coasts she sought out in a peripatetic existence.

Growing up in Nova Scotia, surrounded by descendants of
migrants from Scotland and the North of Ireland (the settle-
ment next to Great Village is named Londonderry!), Bishop's
forebears on both sides were English mariners, some *via* Cape
Breton, others by way of Boston.

HIGH AND ALONE

And Bishop uniquely understands what's special about coast-
lines and islands: remoteness and solitude, and something of
the need for the sea. Of course everyone quotes John Donne
and *No Man is An Island*. But what Elizabeth Bishop actually
gets is that maybe we should allow ourselves to be islands
some of the time, not simply for the sake of being isolated, but
to learn the value of 'aloneness'.

> There is a peculiar quality about being alone, an
> atmosphere that no sounds or persons can ever give.

It is as if…the mind finds its Sea, the wide quiet plane with different lights in the sky and different, more secret sounds. But it appears that we are frightened by the first breaking of its waves at our feet, and now we will never go on voyages of discovery…and never find the islands of the Imagination…Being alone can be fun; alone the mind can do what it wants to. But we can never understand this while we stand on the shore with our backs to the water and cry after our companions. Perhaps we shall never know the companion in ourselves who is with us all our lives, the nearness of our minds at all times to the rare person whose heart quickens when a bird climbs high and alone in the clear air.

So, Elizabeth Bishop's islander/sandpiper mindset, her questing and questioning, are a major influence behind my coasts and islands journey, an encouragement to rediscover that other self, deep down, whose heart quickens at the sound of a kittiwake's cry, the lilt of *The Skye Boat Song*, or the rush of waves retreating on shingle.

9: Achill Island, County Mayo

I think of being young, in the coastguard station.
Those cement cottages with the washing
Swaying in the sea wind.
— Tom Paulin, *The Harbour in the Evening*

DIARY EXTRACTS, LATE MARCH

A new island day surfaces. Rain lashes the cottage windows. Slievemore looms imperious, implacable.

How do you start out on a day so heavy with melancholy, an unanchored slice of time, a morning loosed so far from landfall?

I head out early, waterproofed, face open to stinging rain. Ear-splitting gusts whip & flap my hood, collar, scarf. Same wind that's buffeting ancient mainsails somewhere out on the deep right now.

This island of low cloud, of chained collies, of shoreline kelp, an island of stripped thorn trees, some wrenched by the roots, roots so bog-black they might have journeyed to some Stygian underworld, & back.

By afternoon a few off-course herring gulls will make for a sparse, bleak soundtrack.

This morning I take shelter in the Mission's stone church of desolation, evangelical tracts fluttering when a side-door is wrenched wide by the next gust.

Shut sweet-shops, boarded-up guesthouses, deserted strand car-parks.

We holidayed here decades ago when there was life, still, in the late light evenings. When bulbs lit up the long low hotel front. When my father would take my mother's hand & swirl her into a *Tennessee Waltz* again.

Now it's a stark place of scattered lifeless bungalows waiting for the season, any season, to begin.

A fine, & grave, & quiet place.

Keel Strand: the lone storekeeper readies for another year, likely his last. I watch him through the glass-panelled door, stooped, unsure on a lightweight step-ladder, shifting a rack of floor-mops, a crate of *Calypso* cartons. The lamp-post's *HB Ices* sign has lost its 1960s reds & yellows.

Footmarks in sand: twiglike, delicate, birdlike. No human prints. I've never seen so few people.

Where are the mothers to call children home on summer's-end evenings? What children?

Our Lady of the Assumption: I remember Sundays here as a child. Only sign of a congregation on this wet Lenten Tuesday is lost property in the porch, a single glove (purple stripes with glitter threads), two telescoping umbrellas, one pair of pale blue pearlised rosaries.

In the lower graveyard I read polished granite dedications in two languages. Note the families who lost more than one son, husband, brother, often in the same boat. Such days when such news came. And the whole island would stand on the shore as one, watching the horizon.

They say an island's power is its stranglehold on your soul. There are days you could believe in the walking on water.

When you sleep, finally, on island nights, the sea agitates around your front door, threatens the known edges of your world, wind owl-hoots in chimneys & all you can hear is the low-whispering responsorial of sea-bed lamentations.

Tonight, a moon full to overflowing behind Slievemore: & beyond Keem Bay a long-distance swimmer will pass in the early hours, slip across shipping lanes, crossing & criss-crossing your delta waves.

10: All Points North, or True North

In Japan people don't sleep with heads pointing North,
as that's how the deceased are placed at wakes.

A NORTHERN LITANY

Frontier of loneliness. Dark nights. Melancholia.
Learning the seas: Arctic, Baffin, Greenland,
Norwegian, Barents, Kara, Laptev, Chukchi,
Beaufort & Arctic.
Hsssssh of soundless snowfall, light crunch
of a booted footstep, unearthly silence
before an avalanche. North winds
cut hardest. Hail. On the face. Even in dreams.

North is walrus. Polar bear. Ice-floes.
Icebergs converging on the unsinkable.
Polaris / Pole-Star / North-Star at the Little Bear's tail.
The only guide. *To light, to guard.* All else, darkness.
North is tundra. Unpopulated. Places where nothing
grows. A permafrost wilderness.
North is choppy waters. Extremes. Tempestuous seas.

North is provincial Sundays, reading
Jane Eyre in the rain as light goes.
Vilhelm Hammershøi's mute interiors:
the essence of north.
Those who died by their own hand, buried – a final
sanction – by a churchyard's north wall.
For your penance, a north-facing window.
Northlight. The absence of light.

North is an expedition. A quest.
And if fate allows, a destination.

GRASPING NORTH

North: one of the earliest words in my vocabulary, a marker in my childhood mindscape. How could it have been otherwise, when I looked out north, daily, from the North Antrim coast across the North Channel to our more northerly neighbour? Like so many who identify with 'north', I relished the conflicting awarenesses of both clinging to a vital, wintry 'northernness' and recognising that the centre, the norm, lay elsewhere, outside our 'northern' grasp.

Each year my father drove us south for holidays. To 'the South'. Words that spelled the very opposite of 'north'. 'Holidays' and 'north' just didn't chime with us. Even now, mentions of Arctic cruises hint more at perseverance than pleasure.

Yet my father's brother, Uncle Hugh, had chosen to live in Inverness (57.47°N 4.23°W) on the Moray Firth, north of Aberdeen and its much-sung *Northern Lights*. I would imagine him there in a vista of Austrian peaks dusted by persistent, perpetual snowfalls. Scotland was more 'north' than we were. Scotland was real winter.

In a huge old classroom atlas, I'd trace a finger the length of Loch Ness, count the glens (different tally every time), roll around in my mouth the syllables, the vowels, of Cawdor and Culloden.

I once heard a writer describe her earliest memory, of lying in a pram and recognising her own existence! I recall only the North Channel, our own local subdivision of the North Sea, in invariably northern light, in northernmost weather.

'True North' is, we know, a place we might never reach, but one which remains steadfast in the imagination, a trembling compass-point to strive for: to dream, finally, of understanding the magnetic pull of north.

NORTHLAND

From my ship's bridge
in a next-door-neighbour's tree
I can see all sea routes lead north.
Freezing fog & blizzards from here to Spitzbergen.
Slivers of the Snow Queen's icy mirror that pierce deep.

NORTHERN EXPONENTS

Canadian geographer Louis-Edmund Hamelin claims *north is more than an area, it is a passion* while historian William Morrison suggests that the Canadian North is not a physical region at all, but a place of dreams, of imagination and fantasy.

Though my stamp-album's Canada page showed no snow-laden peaks: only crowned heads, the maple leaf, the excitement of steam trains, sailboats, airplanes and astronauts.

O Canada! Where was my Canada of snowy wilderness and bare expanse? Where were the images of emptiness I wanted to contemplate, the snowscape my wintry mind would understand?

I would find, in fact, on my journey, that Cape Breton's northern coastal tip is farther south than Paris! Where were the snows of my childhood imagination?

NORTHERN LIGHTS

On this side of the Atlantic, way beyond Scotland's northern extremes, Helsinki-born (60.19°N 24.95°E) Tove Jansson (another pre-Melville mobile-library find) captures the pathos, in her *Summer Book*, of going north for winter, a winter of yearning for the brief Scandinavian summer, over almost as soon as begun, with time flying and the Kingdom of North returning again by August, when summer comes suddenly to a standstill, exhausted, drained, defeated.

Yet George Mackay Brown, whose island poetry took me to Orkney, describes those islands' magical essence as *silence, loneliness, and the deep, marvellous rhythms of sea and land, darkness and light.*

Never farther before than John O'Groats and Scrabster ferry port, my crossing into Stromness (58.96°N 3.30°W) by way of the reputedly tempestuous Pentland Firth was visually dramatic but unexpectedly smooth. No hint of the rough-seas experience of wartime sailors crossing to Scapa Flow after the long Thurso train-journey, of Italian POWs taken to Britain's culturally and meteorologically most distant point from Naples; and no hint of the dangers of the old route to Trondheim and Tromso, of the waters that did for *Sir Patrick Spens* on his diplomatic/dynastic mission *to Noroway o'er the foam.*

As for that interplay of *darkness and light*, no hint obviously, in that week, of the almost-darkness-at-noon that rules Orcadian midwinter life, but just enough, at midsummer, of the almost-midnight-sun to open up, for me, a whole Scandinavian world of endlessly yearned-for, yet ephemeral, Tove Jansson summer.

11: On Three Sides

NORTH HOUSE

Our promontory house observes the sea on three sides.
A mansard dwelling that guards its northernness.

Our blue front door, with its summer-bubbled
gloss paint, shrinks a little, shrivels
a little, with each new winter.

Our north-wing corridors are the iciest in history.

This solemn home has witnessed
too many shipwrecks, too few survivors.
The whole house heaves in early hours.

By September saltwater rises above the upper
window-frames, bestowing us with spectacular vistas
of cuttlefish & rainbow scales.

By midday we've tumbled into a blackness
that muffles a tolling parish bell.

When every clock in the house stutters
in synchronous unison, the outboard motor
in the understory is our one salvation.

We rejoice silently, in our frosty northern fashion,
retreating into peaceable, unhazarded midsummers.

12: Metaphorical Oceans

It may be we shall touch the Happy Isles...
— Tennyson, *Ulysses*

Not hard to tell, once you've walked out from the beach's tide-marks into the first breakers, whether the sea in which you're standing is merely symbolic. On the other hand, when I wrote the poem *No Far Shore* in *Late Crossing*, I wasn't thinking of an actual sea journey but an imagined setting-out into unknown waters.

Have I been seeking, I wonder, ever since that first book, my equivalent of Emily Dickinson's *Exultation*, her sense of the thrill of taking to the sea? *The shore is safer but I love to buffet the sea...I love the danger*, she wrote to a friend.

Or do I search, like Elizabeth Bishop, for remote island coves, for buried memories of a first home by the ocean, before some sea-change swamped the decks?

For many writers, the quest isn't exultation or solace but opportunity and challenge: Shakespeare's *There is a tide in the affairs of men* or TH White's more uncertain *One can't tell whether there won't be a tide to catch, some beautiful morning.*

White's tentativeness turns to optimism when the phrase *some beautiful morning* is taken up by C Day Lewis (who spent child-hood summers on Wexford beaches): *It will come soon — one more spring tide to lift / us off...Fortunate they who now can read / their sailing orders as a firm God-speed, / this voyage reaches you beyond the horizon.*

Beyond the horizon to the Ithaca it had taken Odysseus ten

years to get back to, perhaps, the *Ithaka* that is Greek poet CP Cavafy's longed-for destination. He had lived in both Alexandria and Liverpool, and understood sea-faring: *Hope the voyage is a long one...May there be many a summer morning when, | with what pleasure, what joy, | you come into harbours seen for the first time.*

Louis MacNeice (who, as a holidaying child, gazed, from Cushendall beach, at that same Kintyre coastline I would find myself watching all year round) recognises the imperative to set out once again, however late, in one of his last poems, *Thalassa* (the Greek word for 'sea'). And when he writes *By a high star our course is set | Our end is Life. Put out to sea*, we wonder if *Life* is really on the sailing orders.

Just as I remain uncertain about what I do or don't expect to find on this nocturnal poem-journey from my first book.

NO FAR SHORE

It will be winter when I untie
the boat for the last time:
when I double-lock the back door
on an empty house,
go barefoot through bramble
& briar, measure each
stone step to the slipway.

It will be night-time when I row
to the horizon,
steady in North-Star light
the darkened house at my back.

It will be winter when I draw
each oar from the water,
shiver,
& bite the cold from my lip.

from *Late Crossing*

13: In Which I Sing the Praises of Isolated Islets and Sundry Archipelagoes

We who live inland never know anything about islands...
It is in islands there is magic...
It is the island-dweller whose heart leaps and sings.
– Kingsley Porter, American antiquarian
(who disappeared on Inisbofin
off the Connemara coast in 1933)

TO THE ISLANDS

What is it about a piece of land, large or small, desert or rocky, surrounded by waves, that so obsesses some of us? The romance is clearly central to children's fiction. And, as a child, I certainly longed to be washed up on an island, dreamed of building that hut and learning basic survival skills. I would paddle to the farthest rocks at low tide hoping to be cut off, stranded, when the tide would rise. I wanted to be surrounded by water. But still to be rescued before nightfall.

Elizabeth Bishop often holidayed on the Maine coastline with its hundreds of islands and especially, later in life, on North Haven Island. She saw the island's remoteness as paralleling her own sense of isolation, her aloneness in the world, her never-quite-belonging.

...I'd have
nightmares of other islands
stretching away from mine, infinities
of islands, islands spawning islands,
like frogs' eggs turning into polliwogs
of islands...
– Elizabeth Bishop, *Crusoe in England*

ISOLA / ISOLATION

One of the things that draws me to Tove Jansson's writing, in addition to her northern sense, is her love, like Bishop's, of islands. And, in particular, the tiny, rocky Klovharu (60.16°N 25.80°E), her summer escape for decades, as she tells us in her *Notes from an Island* and *The Summer Book*. Her ideal was to arrive in May and not leave until September. Often inaccessible due to sailing conditions, there were even times when it was possible to reach the island but not disembark: inaccessibility as a guarantee of almost perfect isolation.

It's in an island's nature, it's in the very word island, that it should hold itself back from the outside world as much as possible. Islands are loners.

TUESDAY ISLAND

If you set sail on a Monday you'll be on the island
with the morning tide. It's a one-way trip.
White sands, of course, & there's a single *canariensis*
palm tree. Best of all
you'll find yesterday, yesterday, yesterday.

DISAPPEARANCES

And islands can be wilfully elusive, often floating in mist, vivid for a period each day and then, without warning, erased. As with Brian Friel's mysterious island in *Wonderful Tennessee*, a play whose dramatic *inaction* hovers around three contemporary couples waiting on a disused County Donegal pier, a stage set I would be reminded of again and again by sleepy, deserted harbours such as Fresgoe in Caithness, Fethard, County Wexford, or Menemsha on Martha's Vineyard.

Friel's boatman – who never actually materialises – is (like Charon who ferries souls to the underworld) meant to take the couples to a frequently disappearing island, an 'isle of wonder' like Prospero's in *The Tempest*. The play touches on elements of the supernatural from classical and pagan Irish myth, including more than a hint of *Hy-Breasail* (the Celtic equivalent of the *Fortunate Isles*) which only appears once in every seven years.

In an intensely plangent drama of metaphysics, myth, mood and uncanny atmosphere, Friel's characters delve deep into the otherness of islands. A drama of failing to succeed in even setting out, a drama of unattainability.

A STRANGENESS OF ISLANDS

Imagine leaving an island to sail for home, only to find yourself landing on yet another island, identical to the last one, from which, if you set sail again, you arrive at the next, and the next. Mainland permanently beyond reach.

And there are those tricks of light where the island drifts close, recedes, looms close again, and then an hour later is farther away than ever. Island as illusion.

As a child I watched, daily, the Scottish highlands and islands, impossible to tell in northern sea mists which dark peaks belonged to which. And, from Ballycastle seafront, always looked longingly at verdant Rathlin Island (55.29°N 6.19°W) with its famous puffin colony, and its non-mythical but unique (if ubiquitous on the island) Rathlin Golden Hare, whose lighter coat and blue eyes are a localised island mutation that could save a geneticist a long trip to the Galapagos archipelago.

Years later I would discover the almost surreal, stark, stony landscape that is Inis Meáin, the middle Aran Island off the County Clare coast. An island that, despite its rocky barrenness supports a population of 160-ish, though with only four cars when I was there, and, as it was winter, a pub that didn't open until Friday.

Even on small-scale islands there's a good-side/bad-side, maybe north or south side, always, in the local lore, some aspect to be avoided. On Inis Meáin it might be the side farthest from the pier, where a turbine captures the western wind's Atlantic power. The wilder side, with large, unevenly heaped ocean boulders that shift underfoot: a scary experience, even before you notice the stone memorial for someone who met his death on that forbidding stretch of rocks.

My most Inis-Meáin poem (in *Understudies*) borrows its title *Grey Bowl of Heaven* from Antrim Coast poet, Louis MacNeice, whose father grew up on Omey, another island off this same western shore. No Giotto blues for us here; no tourist-postcard technicolour, this far out in the wide, wide ocean.

There can't be many Irish writers, many writers anywhere, though, who aren't captivated by the lure of the island, by the lore of islands.

AN ISLAND ALMANAC

1. Regard the terrain as moonscape. Count the craters.

2. An island watercolourist wouldn't start with a sea-blue wash.

3. Ignore any death rattles: they're invariably east wind leaf-tremblings.

4. Never despair, before too long you'll adopt an islander gait.

5. There's just a lone road, straight to the high cliff, no turning-places.

6. *The isle is full of noises, / Sounds, and sweet airs that give delight* (Caliban)

7. Sacramental: first time you swim off an island, it's a baptism into a new faith.

8. Hold on, is there even a ladder on this island?

9. There's always a footprint: despite appearances, you're never alone.

10. Island skies will fall piece by piece, leaving only clouds suspended.

14: Island Notes

The islands haven't shifted since last summer,
even if I like to pretend they have –
drifting, in a dreamy sort of way...
– Elizabeth Bishop, North Haven

ORANGE PEEL CAFÉ

Martha's Vineyard: an island of artists, musicians, politicians, an island of sunshine and five lighthouses. Though even in summer – well, late spring – a landscape strangely stark, roads lined with stripped white oaks. I sail early evening from Woods Hole Harbour with spectacular twilight weaving between black skerries and submerged rocks. An hour later I arrive on 'MV' in complete sea-and-land-darkness, until out of nowhere on Edgartown's edge there's a brightly lit cantina and the enticement of pizza herbs on the air.

Driving next morning to Aquinnah Light (41.33°N 70.85°W) I shiver at the white treescape's coldness. By the airfield I recall news updates on the search for John Kennedy in that same land-and-sea blackness as last night's, his plane (with his wife and sister-in-law on board) destined for this field on West Tisbury Road. And think of him in night-flying disorientation, not helped perhaps by fragmented coastlines and clusters of smaller islands, or, seemingly, by Aquinnah, East Chop, Edgartown or by any of MV's lighthouses.

Aquinnah Light, operational and blinking red through today's blinding sunlight, has been rolled back several times in its 200-year-history (and moved again just recently, keeping it safe from another 100 years' worth of coastal erosion). A nearby cluster of shops and shacks has (just about) opened for the season.

My notes, from that spring morning, scribbled at a folding table outside the Orange Peel Café, puzzle over what local 'youth' do over long, bleak, island-winter months on small winding island roads that look, today, tourist-cute as though they've never seen winter. The unparalleled sleepy beauty of Menemsha's unseasonally sky-blue, sea-blue, *Blue-Bayou*-blue harbour images jostling aside memories of teenage *ennui* in my own stunningly scenic, but deserted-out-of-season coastal town.

TRUE ISLANDS

Jacquish (43.71°N 70.00°W): a short rowboat trip from the end of Bailey Island, off Orr's Island, linked by bridge, like Sebascodegan Island, to Harpswell. Stepping stones. A necklace. Like Elizabeth Bishop's *infinities of islands*. And yet if islands are linked to each other by bridge or causeway, accessible regardless of season, of weather, can they still claim islands' aloofness, an island psyche?

Intriguingly, psychoanalyst CJ Jung, who identified 'the island' as one of the 'regions of danger' threatening his 'archetypal hero', visited and lectured here on Jacquish in 1936, though shortly after the opening of a bridge that had actually eliminated that island/danger correlation.

(Bailey Island Bridge: only cribstone bridge in the world, apparently. Reports of there having been one other cribstone bridge, in Scotland, are unconfirmed. Perhaps one of those phenomena, like *Brigadoon*, like Brian Friel's disappearing island, that only appear every seven, or every 100 years?)

Nothing visible in today's mist but a lone house, vague, tentative, like the opening sequence in a ghost story. One you could step into. Step through, scene by scene: tether the boat; watch house lights go out, one by one, in misty dark. No one answers the bell-pull…

IN THE MARITIMES

Prince Edward Island (freeway signs simply say PEI) is connected to the mainland by an eight-mile bridge. Not as long as the one on which I crossed over Louisiana's Lake Pontchartrain a year ago, the longest, over water, in the world: this is only the longest over water that's ice-covered for part of the year, they say. Exhilarating, though, to be suspended in nothingness for such a long stretch.

An island of green fields and churches (of which, surprisingly, the largest in the Kensington area is the Catholic church, looking like something transplanted miraculously from Umbria, but clapboard-built!) And endless fertile rich red soil, responsible for the island's vast potato production.

PEI's most celebrated inhabitant was Lucy Maud Montgomery whose *Anne of Green Gables* was a childhood favourite, so I find myself *en route* now to the real-life 'Green Gables' farmstead (46.49°N 63.39°W) that belonged to her cousin David Macneill (namesake of my Glenravel great-uncle). Montgomery's maternal grandfather was a Macneill, but what I didn't know was that her grandmother was a Woolner from Dunwich in Suffolk, or from what's left of Dunwich, once an international port, the size of London in the 14th century, which fell Atlantis-like victim to coastal erosion, and whose submerged underwater streets, priories and mediaeval alleyways have troubled my imagination, and my writing, since first discovering its history on an Aldeburgh coast autumn residency some years ago.

PROUD BEARING

One particular quest on Cape Breton Island is to cross Seal Island Bridge, on Trans Canada Highway 105, to Boularderie Island, then to Great Bras d'Or Lake, (an 'arm of gold' only if you catch it in a certain setting sun) and find McNeil Beach Lighthouse, which I've been warned is inaccessible. But I find a path through trees, along a spookily unpeopled stretch of jagged, wooded shoreline and past a couple of abandoned houses where I nonetheless feel certain I'm not alone.

And there it is: a baby lighthouse (just 33 feet high), a small bundle of a lighthouse, red and white, nestling under that great bridge, looking alone and lost in mist and fine rain, but still holding what I recognise as proud McNeill bearing. And I buy, at *Colaisde na Gàidhlig* (The Gaelic College) at St. Ann's (46.21°N 60.60°W), a CD of Scottish/Cape-Breton music by the *Barra McNeils*: my own County Antrim McNeills came from Barra in the Western Isles.

Separated from the rest of Nova Scotia by the Strait of Canso's North Atlantic waters until 1955 (but now joined by the Canso Causeway), Cape Breton was a true island when Elizabeth Bishop came here in 1947 (it's that year's summer-house I've come in search of), just as it was when her homesick mother trained as a teacher here in the 1890s.

Shoreline unsettling and disquieting. Around the coves I find only an eerie silver light, expanses of glassy water, all verging on the uncanny. White beaches, patterned stones, pale washed-out twigs, all surrounded by dark, gloomy tree clumps. Wooden shacks leaning heavily windward from constant gale-batterings. Copses that seem to hold their secrets close.

A SLOW MAINE SUNDAY

A fishing community and summer colony: Bristol's Captain Martin Pring 'discovered' North Haven (44.13°N 68.88°W) in 1603, even though it was long part of Penobscot Abenaki Indian territory, 'christening' it, with neighbouring Vinal-haven, as 'the Fox Islands'.

As I chug sea-miles out across Penobscot Bay on a wet Sunday morning ferry, I think of Elizabeth Bishop on this same crossing, imagining herself sailing across some underworld river to meet up with her recently departed friend Robert Lowell, whose summer place in Castine could be seen from the bay and from her island hideout.

It's a slow Maine Sunday, a Sunday of low visibility. Alighting after a thick-misted hour (Bishop's mists seem to have been more persistent, according to her 1979 North Haven poem *The Foggy Summer*) I watch the last wisp evaporate in spring light as local librarian Kate Quinn meets me at the ramp to drive me the length and breadth of her island, filling me in on the way with news, and backstories, of the island's inhabitants, both 'year-rounds' (including her own family) and the island's celebrated but reclusive 'summer people'. And the complex mutual symbiosis between them, as well as changing economic, demographic, and vacationing patterns. Kate's lived here all her life, as her people have done for generations.

SABINE FARM

Last stop, Kate takes me to Sabine Farm, Bishop's summer home for many years (yes, a wooden verandah house just like her maternal grandparents' home in Great Village, Nova Scotia, and just down through the trees, there's a small beach not unlike the one on Cobequid Bay behind Great Village).

In all that time spent exploring houses, ponds, harbours, driveways, farmtracks and an airstrip, we see no one (population 350). But I begin to feel like I belong here: perhaps it's the intimate sense of belonging that Bishop bestows on all of us through her North Haven Journal.

Perhaps, too, it's Kate's ease with enquiring strangers, her love of her home place. The reserve and generosity of the islander who doesn't need the other third-of-a-billion Americans a ferry-ride away.

We're definitely on what's proudly, comfortably, thought of as 'island time' here, and the only sign of life is the quiet bustle (and the welcome) in the General Store. And the smell of vanilla coffee. Still puzzling, though, over what young year-rounders do in coastal/island communities when summer ends, as it did for us in Cushendall every September.

After hours together Kate leaves me in the closed library (which opens once a week, on Wednesday afternoons) to pass time until the evening ferry back to Rockland, and simply pull the door shut as I go!

Some islands can gift you a magic day and this is one. With the bonus of book browsing. Bishop, on library visits, mentions in her North Haven journal that she *loved Lord Jim in the Children's Room*. I'm off to explore!

15: Cloud Watch

...Out of the light evolved the morning blooms,

Who, then, evolved the sea-blooms from the clouds
Diffusing balm in that Pacific calm?
– Wallace Stevens, Sea Surface Full of Clouds

1. EAVESDROPPING

Parents whisper about H-bombs, mushroom clouds,
Cold War implications.

Children hear only talk of fluffy sheep, cotton candy,
a giant's eiderdown.

The Bellevue Zoo giraffe hears the whole sky
echo a short distance from his ear.

2. CLOUDBANK OF MEMORY

Scanning the blue yonder from the side path:
towering dark pines, Monterey cypress,
unrelenting tree cover.

Just once a dark mass passes
on the wrong side of the sky.
A plane, hovering like a dark angel. I swear
I see a swan's head & neck
in the cockpit. No one believes me.

In February the house is eclipsed
from morning until night. Sky is getting in the way.

I ask my father what you'd find inside a cloud.

Rainy days, he says, *any God's number of them.*
We have two budgies, & a cloudfish that circles the
bowl.
Neighbours ask where we bought the cloudfish.

I always draw the infant sizes in right hand corners,
using a cloud-stencil for sharp outlines.
Then fill in sky-blue perfectly up to the line.
Cloudlets never reach second grade.

I can't ever imagine a whole family of clouds.
Or a cloud-sister.
There is only ever one child. A solitary.

High formations follow our Hillman Hunter
all the long, long way from the Ring of Kerry, back
to our own Antrim Coast. Each perfectly framed
in the car's rear window.

I decorate their names in my gilt-edged notebook.

Cloud-samples prism onto schoolroom-blue walls
as the educational globe whirls on its spindle.

I long for those clouds to speak, to send me a message.

3. A CLOUD CEILING

…is blue-glass, is translucent, too high for mortals.

4. THE CLOUD-LIFE MUSEUM ON BOTANIC

There's a craft room for cut-outs. The air is Giotto-
blue.

Pay your money & guess the weight of a cloud.
You must use the 3-D glasses provided
for the whole duration of Cloud Trail adventure.

In the basement you can chart cirrus-cloud
mythologies, life cycles, ancient genealogies.

On Thursdays we rearrange the diorama scenery.

Children are invited to participate, swap shapes
in & out of place. Here, clouds are lumbering & noisy.

Exhibit One has been stolen. So there's
a misty fourth plinth waiting to be filled. Please
forward concepts for due consideration.

5. CUMULUS FACTS

Saturday's cloud: heavy with weightlessness, absence.

You step off stratus into an atmospheric abyss
each morning you wake.

The one I keep in my pocket has a knot tied
in one corner, monogrammed initials in the other.

The eye of the cloud. Beware. Bloodshot, dilation,
veins.

The noblest leave their interiors to science. Nothing
shows on X-ray. Autopsies rarely reveal
true cause of death.

6. CLOUD CAPTURE

Force one into a Kilner jar, toss in the air,
high as you can,
watch it rotate into orbit. Aeons from now
the message will be misunderstood in another galaxy.

16: Into the Maelstrom

The bottom of the sea is cruel.
– Hart Crane, *Voyages*

Cargo: 110 bags of letter mail, 425 bags of parcel post, 1000 rail parcels, 2 tons of baggage, 6 boxes of fish, 5 hampers of laundry, 6 drums, 3 bales, 5 cases, 1 parcel, 55 cartons of footwear, 1 skip, 520 sanitary pipes, 2 trusses of textiles (crates), 14 tea chests full of sundries, 2 boxes of tyre covers, 160 bags of brush blanks.

CROSSING

I wonder whether all those raised by the sea but living in a city experience the same sea-fever I do when, driving 380 miles north from London, I catch the first pewter glimpse of Solway light at Gatehouse of Fleet that tells me Stranraer's less than an hour away. Stranraer: with its inevitable sense of being – almost – within sight of the Antrim coastline and home.

An exultation at the prospect of embarking that remains undimmed after hundreds of fair and storm-tossed crossings, but always tinged with the memory, not mine, but family memory handed on from a time before I was born, of the sinking of the MV *Princess Victoria* on that short Stranraer-Larne route.

17:55, 30/1/53: Gale warning: *gale warnings are in operation for the sea areas, Iceland, Faroes, Fair Isle, Bailey, Rockall, Shannon, Fastnet, Malin, Irish Sea and Lundy.*

Summer evenings through childhood, as we ordered ice-cream sundaes on the terraced lawn of Green's Café on Carnlough Bay, it was difficult to forget that one of the two 'lady proprietors', Miss Ada Prior, had drowned on that fateful crossing.

A SHIP'S CLOCK

A ship's clock is stopped and time at sea stands still. On 31st January 1953 MV *Princess Victoria* perished in the North Channel, between Stranraer and Larne, with the loss of 133 lives.

In September 1949 my parents had moved into a house named *Glendun* on Limerick Point in Dalriada, Cushendall. They slept and woke to the dreamy divination of North Channel waters over the ensuing years. What might they have been doing, on an unassuming Saturday at the end of January? My mother talked later of search beams in the sky in the days and weeks that followed as bodies continued to be washed ashore.

But of that day, of that late afternoon and evening, I have no sense, not just of the mood (was it a Kennedy 'where were you?' moment for our coastal community?), but of how the news arrived. No bulletins, then, interrupting television programmes. No TVs to speak of. When did they first hear? Did they switch on to listen for radio news on the hour as my father would later do consistently down the years? Described as a generation's *Titanic*, the disaster must have called up deep sonic echoes and shock-waves.

SKYLIGHT

Friday night, the night before the tragedy, was my parents' usual film night: Moyle Cinema on Mill Street. Maybe Ingrid Bergman, whom my mother loved, in *The Bells of St. Mary's*? Or *Gaslight*? Maybe a new release: *Gentlemen Prefer Blondes*, out earlier that very month but how quickly did the Moyle show the latest releases? Perhaps my father bought Rowntree's Fruit Jellies or Fry's Five Centres, and two Cantrell & Cochrane minerals. (Not that they drank mineral water back then: what our American cousins called sodas - lemonade, orangeade, ice-cream soda – were referred to in Ireland as 'minerals'.)

Capable of transporting 1500 passengers, plus cargo, and with

54 berths, MV *Princess Victoria* was a roll-on / roll-off ferry, built in 1947 at Dumbarton, 60 miles north-east of us across the Firth of Clyde, and the fourth ship to bear the name, her immediate predecessor having been sunk in the Humber estuary by a German World War II mine.

That last is the sort of fact my mother would have counted a troubling omen: just as she would have regarded a single magpie. In her last months of life, almost five decades later, we were still saluting, both of us, chivalrously, our black-and-white avian neighbours on the roadside, on frequent trips between her cancer treatments, at Belfast's Belvoir Hospital, and Glendun Nursing Home.

In all that time I got to spend with my mother (having left my London home to be with her through her illness) it hadn't occurred to me – until writing this, in fact – how the name of her final 'home' was also the name of her first 'newly wed' home, *Glendun*, at Limerick Point.

That first *Glendun* house had an attic skylight. My best friend, Angela, in *Glenaan*, the house next door, also had a skylight. We found, as children, that if we stood on tea-chests in her attic and raised the window, we could look out and see Garron Point, then imagine the series of bays and headlands you rounded on Sunday afternoon drives, until the imagination ran out at Larne Harbour: the *far shore* that MV *Princess Victoria* did not reach on that 31st January.

GUILLOTINE DOOR

07:45, 31/1/53: MV *Princess Victoria* leaves Stranraer harbour, captained by 55-year-old James Ferguson. The vessel carried 44 tons of cargo, 51 crew and 128 passengers.

The ship sails despite a severe gale warning in place from the previous evening. Due perhaps to Loch Ryan's deceptive calm, that long inlet well sheltered from the North Channel.

The Guillotine, an extra door that apparently always took 'too long' to raise and lower, isn't in place. Too long, but it might have offered protection when waves began breaking over the stern doors. (*Guillotine*: another word that would have unsettled my omen-conscious mother.)

08:45: In the teeth of an 80 mph gale, Captain Ferguson decides to return to Stranraer.

> *08:55*: My father leaves the house to walk to work in the village (he worked mornings-only on Saturdays). The garage smells of oil & spray paint. By nine, he's thinking about his work schedule up to lunchtime. Lynn's shop window on Bridge Street is brightly lit for a wintry morning. Lizzie McKillop wraps Cheddar blocks in greaseproof paper. Across the road Gus Lynn completes his diary for January: *fairly uneventful month,* he might write.

09:00: Turning manoeuvre means stern doors take full force of storm & high seas. Doors buckle. Crew unable to close.

09:46: Morse message received: *Hove-to off mouth of Loch Ryan. Vessel not under command. Urgent assistance of tugs required.* List of 15 degrees in vessel.

> *10:15*: Wind howls in the chimneys. My mother clearing dishes. Perhaps the rose-patterned china breakfast set (a wedding present). Thinking, maybe, of postponing, weatherwise, a late-morning bus-trip to Cargan to visit McNeill aunts, our family dressmakers until my father bought my mother the Singer whose counterpoint of treadle and gentle clickety-clack was the background to childhood evenings. Or perhaps she's already at the top of Dalriada, the Coast Road bus-stop, opposite the doctor's surgery. Perhaps she's chatting to the bus-driver. About the sudden weather.

10:32: SOS transmission: ... --- ... / ... --- ... / ... --- ...

10:34: Morse signal received by destroyer HMS *Contest* from *Princess Victoria* four miles north-west of Corsewall Point (55.00°N 5.15°W).

11:00: Portpatrick lifeboat, *Jeannie Spiers*, dispatched, given inaccurate location.

11:09: HMS *Contest* dispatched.

11:37: Starboard list of 35 degrees. HMS *Launceston Castle*, frigate *en route* to Derry, is first on the scene but has to leave when condensers become contaminated by salt.

12:00: Gales, force 9 to 12. Poor visibility prevents HMS *Contest* seeing the sinking ship.

12:25: Ship's clock stops. Power lost.

12:52: Starboard engine-room flooded. List is now 60 degrees.

> *13:00*: My father has returned to the house. Has news come through on Lynn's phone? Has my schoolteacher aunt driven the nine miles from Cargan down to Cushendall in her new Volkswagen as soon as she heard? Had my parents planned a Ballymena shopping Saturday, the pattern, later, of my childhood? My father collecting my mother in Glenravel? But perhaps she hasn't gone. Has stayed home and kept a fire lit against the storm outside, against the long, shuttered-in after-noon ahead.

13:08: Engines have stopped. Morse: *We are preparing to abandon ship.*

13:35: Crew sights the Irish coast.

13:40: Passengers ordered on to deck.

13.58: Final Morse signal five miles east of Copeland Islands: *On beam end.*

14:00: Order given to abandon ship

An RAF Hastings aircraft has been assisting rescues off Barra, 160 miles north, and Lewis, a further 80. Doesn't reach the scene until 15:31. Also dispatched: cattle ship *Lairdsmoor*, trawler *Eastcotes*, coastal oil tanker *Pass of Drumochter*, coastal cargo ship *Orchy*.

All women and children safely boarded in first lifeboat. Capsizes on impact with water. There are only 44 survivors from the sinking. All men. Only 100 out of 133 bodies ever recovered, some as far away as Isle of Man (54.32°N 4.09°W).

There were a total of 531 weather-based fatalities throughout the UK on that day, a quarter of them in the *Princess Victoria* tragedy, the largest ferry disaster in UK waters. Later the *Herald of Free Enterprise* would claim 193 off Zeebrugge in 1987, MS *Estonia* would take 852 lives in the Baltic in 1994.

RMS *Titanic*'s final loss, 41 years earlier, had been 1514.

FAMILY HISTORIES

They called the *Princess Victoria*'s sinking 'our *Titanic*', on our stretch of the coast, in our small town of coastal and deep-sea mariners. Accounts always seem to list the 'important' people who died – as they do with the *Titanic* – but our community counted people who were known locally, the ordinary workers, crew and catering, from Stranraer and Larne, and those who worked, or were visiting, in Scotland or England and might have been coming home that Saturday, as I would be so many times a year, however many years later.

But Belfast's *Titanic* was already our family's *Titanic*, though my Belfast-born mother would never refer, locally, in our predominantly Catholic glen, to the fact that her father, William Reilly, had been a shipyard worker, meaning, obviously, that he was a Protestant, given the Belfast shipyards' religious bias: in his case a Church of Ireland southerner from County Cavan.

But it was William Reilly's falling in love with a Catholic girl from the Glens that saved his life: on board RMS *Titanic* as far as her sea-trials in Liverpool, and selected to accompany the ship to New York as one of a small group of fitters, he quit in Liverpool, and came home to Mary McNeill from Cargan, eloping by night to avoid parental disapproval (on both sides) of 'mixed' marriages. My McNeill great-grandparents pursued them as far as Ballymena and brought them home to Glenravel where they were married in Mary's local Catholic parish church.

William Reilly went on to bring up their children as Catholics and chose to live in a Catholic/Nationalist enclave known as the Short Strand, despite Belfast's extreme sectarian divisions. And he's buried beside Mary in Glenravel's Catholic cemetery, though he'd always known that embracing his wife's faith, in his lifetime, would cost him his shipyard livelihood.

-.-. --.- -.. *vs* ... ---...

So you grow up knowing that your grandfather, whom no one talks about but without whom you wouldn't exist, helped build the unsinkable *Titanic*, and could have died in icy waves on the far side of the Atlantic, despite radio operators Harold Bride and Jack Phillips sending CQD (-.-. --.- -..) messages, the old Marconi code, discontinued not long after that fateful night in 1912. In which case he might have been laid to rest in Halifax, Nova Scotia, rather than Glenravel. Or, more likely, left, like so many, on the 12,000-ft-deep sea-bed.

And you grow up knowing that practically anyone you knew locally could have been on the stricken *Princess Victoria*, as radio operator David Broadfoot from Stranraer went under with his last of fifty-four SOS (... --- ...) messages on a gale-swept 1953 Saturday afternoon.

And still you can't keep away from the sea and its unknown hazards, from crossings and re-crossings, from dreaming horizons and destinations, and from a strange sharp sense of your own family's past when you turn from Stair Drive onto Stranraer's Cairnryan Road after those 400-plus road miles from London, and pass the house that was Captain James Ferguson's until Saturday 31st January 1953 when, like *Titanic*'s Captain Edward Smith on Monday 15th April 1912, he went down with his vessel.

17: Shortwave / Longwave

CQD DE MGY, 41.46 NORTH, 50.14 WEST
– Jack Phillips, *Titanic* radio operator

('MGY' was *Titanic*'s call-sign; Marconi's 'CQD' signal, often referred to as 'come quickly, danger' actually stands for 'CQ', i.e. *sécu(rité)* or 'safety' in French, plus D, for *détresse* ('distress'). As the situation deteriorated Phillips also added the newer signal, 'SOS'.)

Late at night, under covers to drown out crashing sea-sounds, you'd switch over, before Luxembourg's soporific *End of the Day*, to the *00:48 Shipping Forecast*, its northward litany – *Malin, Herbrides, Fair Isle, Faroes* a familiar liturgy as important as prayer, as *guide of the wanderer*, for those *thrown on life's surge*.

And he spent a long time watching
From his lonely wooden tower...
– Leonard Cohen, *Suzanne*

INTO YOUR HANDS...

Guglielmo Marconi's proudest possession: not the 1909 *Nobel Prize for Physics* but the gold tablet presented to him by 600 *Titanic* survivors in gratitude for the invention that brought the RMS *Carpathia* to their rescue. His dying wish: to find, as Thomas Alva Edison had thought he might find, a wavelength between shortwave and longwave that would communicate beyond physics: in Marconi's case, to hear the final notes of the *Titanic*'s orchestra, to hear Jesus's last words on the cross.

FIRST UTTERANCE

Growing up knowing our Antrim coast had hosted the first commercial application of the Italian-Irish inventor's genius (relaying Rathlin lighthouse keepers' shipping observations *via* Ballycastle to Lloyds of London, with significant commodity-broking implications), I shouldn't have been surprised to find Marconi had explored most of my chosen coasts on both sides of the Atlantic a century ahead of me. He had holidayed at his grandfather's castle in County Wexford as a boy. And later had located sea's-edge wireless stations at Cornwall's Poldhu, Glace Bay on Cape Breton Island, Flat Holm Island near Cardiff, Lochboisdale on South Uist, Crookhaven in County Cork and at Wellfleet on Cape Cod's edge.

Perhaps Marconi's choice of Cape Cod's eastern shore was influenced by *Walden* author, Henry David Thoreau, a frequent visitor to nearby Highland Lighthouse (42.03°N 70.06°W), who had identified it as a place where *a man could stand and put America behind him.*

In 1903, just five years after that first Ballycastle signal had arrived across seven miles of stormy Rathlin Sound, Marconi allowed President Roosevelt and Edward VII to exchange diplomatic Morse pleasantries, between his transatlantic Poldhu and Wellfleet stations.

Expecting to find Cape Cod brightly suffused with white light as in Edward Hopper's Highland Lighthouse paintings, and to gaze meaningfully towards the Antrim Glens, or Poldhu or Lochboisdale, across 3000 miles of North Atlantic Ocean (all invisible anyway below an eighth of the earth's curvature, beyond a seemingly flat horizon), I was met with a genuine Cornwall/Rathlin/North-Uist of a day. *Visibility zero* as the late-night shipping litany would put it, a drizzled, foggy reminder of why Marconi's signalling invention has come to matter more than prayer.

18: Wavesounds

Listen: a fourworded wavespeech: seesoo, hrss, rsseeis,
ooos. Vehement breath of waters amid seasnakes,
rearing horse, rocks. In cups of rocks it slops: flop, slap: bounded in
barrels. And, spent, its speech ceases.
It flows purling, widely flowing, floating foampool,
flower unfurling.
– James Joyce, Ulysses

SEA-LEGS

I was born to the beat of waves.
Lungs filled early with sea air & possibility.
Early March & the East Wind cried.
Windows were opaque with salt.
A sea-world awaiting me.

SEA-SENSE

Manageable words were four letters.
Wave. Tide. Calm. Land.
Later words were unintelligible.
Multitudinous phonemes, sibilants.
Complete sentences, every day a dizzying
battle of submerged syllables.
Oystercatcher. Jellyfish. Sea-anemone.
Bladderwrack. Archipelago.

A SHORT HISTORY OF WAVE-MOTION

The wave that began the morning I was born
is now in another galaxy:
a swell that had no beginning,
tiny lappings at first,
no knowledge then of oceans,

shipwrecks,
arbitrary drownings.

CANTICLE: STAR OF THE SEA

℣

Limpid wave, waves of our fathers, motherwave,
wave beyond the lost headlands.
Night-sky waves, the darkest wave, the wave
that washes over our cardinal-red doorstep overnight.
Ice-laden waves, a wave's backstory,
the over-ambitious breakers,
doomed waves of the seven seas.
The wave that clings tightest to a rusted anchor.
Wave wreckage, anticipated wave, timely wave,
oh, fishbowl wave!

℟ *Pray for us.*

℣

The wave that comes out of nowhere at a *speed of knots.*
Wave museum, porcelain wave so bluely preserved,
the tang of waves in July. Lovesick wave,
the unmapped wave, terminal wave, wave soliloquy.
Epic wave, essence of wave, a Cloud-9 wave,
the trembling wave inside the belly of a fish.
The orchestral wave so powerful you proposed.

℟ *Pray for us.*

℟ *Pray for us, now & at the hour of our death.*

SLEEP-WAVES

Virginia Woolf and I have some significant first memories in
common. As a child she's lying half-asleep / half-awake in the
nursery at St. Ives *hearing the waves breaking, one, two, one, two,
and sending a splash of water over the beach; and then breaking, one,*

90

two, one, two, behind a yellow blind. It is of hearing the blind draw its little acorn across the floor as the wind blew the blind out…

Clearly the sea's hypnotic power stayed with Woolf, playing a leading part in her first 'psychological' novel, *The Voyage Out*, and in *To the Lighthouse*, with the breakers she heard as a child inspiring her 'poem-novel' *The Waves*.

NOT WAVING…

Of the two dozen or so Iris Murdoch novels that I studied many years ago, the one that stays with me most is her 1978 Booker-winning *The Sea, the Sea*, with – among so much coastal territory and experience – this dramatic moment of going under:

> …my body was aware that no swimming could take place in that vortex. I felt as if my neck was breaking as I looked up to see a dome of dark faintly translucent green, the wave above me. I was choking and swallowing water, absorbed in the one task of getting another breath. At the same time I was able to think: this is the end.

Such intensity of observation can surely only have come from an author who not only obsessed about the sea but had experienced the physicality of going under once, twice…

INTERROGATORY

Is there anything out there tonight?
A Russian trawler, a submarine,
a functional lighthouse, sharks, even a sea-horse?
What if it's one vast bowl of absence
beyond this window,
nothing but waves inching
into sleep patterns? How close
is the nearest shark right now?

DISCOVERY

Every tide is wave & non-wave,
sine & cosine. At what age
did I know the recurrent *swishings*
below my bedroom window
were also treacherous walls of water
that could take down
ships & sailors,
cargoes,
travellers, dreamers,
down fathoms to the ocean floor?

WAVES OF TORY

An age of innocence.
Parochial Dance Hall evenings
of that Gaeltacht summer:
over-waves, under-waves,
fingertips touching,
bowing of heads, the rhythms,
wavelines forming,
re-forming,
& always on the wave's crest
somewhere at the back of my mind
a storm-tossed frightened currach
off a stony island coast.

LONG-DISTANCE SUMMER

Watching the waves roll in,
then I watch 'em roll away again.
I'm sitting at the signpost.
To where?

TROUBLE AT SEA

The seabed underfoot
has been quickening of late.
Air-bubbling a little more frenetically.

You choose your oxygen with care.
You've become expert at rising to the surface
avoiding the bends,
you were always good at leaving the scene.

Minnows are gliding nose to tail.

WAVE-FORMS

Calculated to numb the past,
my mother's sine-wave ECT sessions
at Holywell Hospital failed to obliterate
the ache for those lost parents,
the sadness that trailed her
through the family seashore years,
caught up in the end, found her again.
Keep running, my gentle mother,
I hear myself whisper, *Stay ahead.*
But waves are lapping at her heels,
overtaking her.
My gentle mother.

19: Leaving Barra

HIGHLANDS AND ISLANDS

What is it, then, I suffer from, when deprived of coastal gaze, what is it that makes coastal light (at Point Lobos above Big Sur, or Bras d'Or Lake on Cape Breton, or Loch Ryan in Galloway) such a much-needed fix? Or gave the Brighton horizon such meaning at the end of a first London winter away from the Antrim coast?

Why the longing, when you're never more than 70 miles from the sea anywhere in Britain? Or when holidays, and years of literary festivals and writers' residencies, have kept me in continual touch with tides, tidelines, and salt-spray?

In fact, on this itinerary, Felixstowe, Swansea, Skye, Cobh, Hook and others were re-visits. And Scotland (I'd been as far as Skye in the west and Thurso in the north before) felt like home anyway, having grown up with Fyfe, McNeill and McIlwaine heritage, in the Antrim Glens among McDonnells, McAlisters, Stewarts and McIntoshes, with Gaelic (Scots or Irish) placenames and Scottish songs on the coastal air.

No one can determine now whether the airs of *The Skye Boat Song* or *Westering Home* originated in Donegal or Antrim, or due north of Cushendall on Islay or Skye, or in the chain of Western Isles from Barra to Lewis, to-and-from which so many Irish families transmigrated for generations, the Barra McNeils descending originally from a Tyrone O'Neill clan chief. So I included the highlands and islands in my itinerary knowing I had lived and breathed Scotland from an early age.

And reading of Tove Jansson's Finland had, at least, prepared me for Orkney's bright midnights: as *Woodbrook* author, David Thomson's *Nairn in Darkness and Light* had already introduced me to the Moray Firth.

WESTERN EDGE

But nothing, not even a Moray Firth sunset at Findhorn, or Orkney's mild landscape, or hilly Skye, readied me for the Western Isles' wild, stark sparseness: a fogbound single dwelling at the end of a spit of land with no other habitation for miles; track-roads on Vatersay that petered out for no apparent reason; long causeways with otter warning signs between what were once separate islands; deserted grassed-over outcrops that might or might not be inhabited, or grazed; just three cars waiting to take the daily ferry to the next island; a mail van arriving with a single letter from Barra to Eriskay.

Not even the dazzling improbability of a lily covered inland mountain tarn high above Lochinver, or the Aegean blue calm of Loch Eireboll, could begin to match the scattered Hebridean jigsaw of skerries, moorland, lochs and small islands – each morphing almost undetectably into the other.

Or begin to compare with the interminable Atlantic horizon on a silver midnight, just after the longest day, and hours since the readings and music at Taigh Chearsabhagh had ended, a momentary vision of the longed-for *far shore*, of *Hy-Breasail*, of *Isles of the Blest,* that would vanish, surely, for some magical number of years.

WESTERING HOME

Visiting the island of Barra was meant to feel like coming home, after family lore in which exile from that place weighed heavily. (Painter James McNeill Whistler claimed Barra heritage too, though genealogical enthusiasts have since shown his ancestors were South Carolina McNeills of a different clan, migrated from Taynish in Argyll.)

If being there on Barra (56.99°N 7.48°W), *under the high and comfortless mountain* of Robinson Jeffers's sad poem, had a revelation for me, it was the starkness that caused so many McNeils to leave for distant shores. Despite their chiefs being noted among the rare good landlords, conditions were such that the chief's elder son, Gilleonan, migrated with 370 of the clan to Cape Breton in 1803.

But Barra showed me the mesmeric lure of the horizon at sunset with its promised end to hard times: even if those Barra McNeils were to discover, at Lake Bras d'Or in Cape Breton, or among the Antrim Glens, new places of equal beauty but of equally severe hardship. Even if they were to find in themselves an unquenchable longing there, to be back home.

20: Grim Sentinels

> *Darkness reigns at the foot of a lighthouse.*
> – Japanese proverb

LODESTONE

There's the pull of the ocean itself, of promontories and precipices, inlets and miles-long shorelines, of unreliable vanishing points.

But there's also that magnetic attraction we experience for the lighthouse, grim sentinel of another world, marking the end-limits of one element and the beginnings of another. And inevitably, a fascination for those whose lives are lived out within such aloof and vital markers.

Growing up so close to the sea, late nights were the time to watch those small, phased, mesmerising lights from a bedroom window. And to dwell, particularly on stormy nights, on the thought that there was someone alone out there, awake all night as you gradually surrendered to sleep, looking out *for those in peril on the sea.*

Towers have their own fascination: hence their prevalence as a literary archetype (as CJ Jung might have told his Jacquish, Maine, audience). There's one at the centre of my home village of Cushendall, the Curfew Tower, a relic of an improving 19th-century landlord's attempt to add law and order to his education and health provisions.

I had always imagined the lighthouse as a version of that familiar Cushendall edifice (itself a later manifestation of the Celtic round tower) with a staircase winding up from floor to floor, from room to smaller room.

But we knew that a lighthouse – we'd only ever seen the outsides on family holidays, and no peekable windows – was a tower with 'inner workings', mediaeval mystery combined with mechanical magic and optical invention: a symbol in itself for sure, but a vital sign to those up to 30 nautical miles away.

THE WORKINGS

The sheer size of lighthouse bulbs first struck me on a visit to Suffolk's Southwold Lighthouse: since when I've realised just how much depended on the lamp, the Fresnel lenses (often ten-foot-tall housings of multiple lenses that could transmit those 30-mile light-beams) and the winding mechanisms.

I've worked the starting-handle-type crank (at Kinnaird Head near Fraserburgh, and at Cape Cod) that rewinds the clock-weights to start their 30-minute descent again, slowly rotating the lens itself by means of a series of gears and cogs. And I've often wondered how it must feel to have to do that again eighteen-or-so times in a nine-hour shift. (In Tiree's Skerryvore Lighthouse, where the keeper on duty slept in a circular bedroom with the winch-cable passing through the floor, it was said he could perform all his duties without getting out of bed.)

VOCATION

Those who chose the lighthouse life – ordinary men, often fathers of families in the locality – had the status of secular monks on their four-week shifts. Unlike seamen who swapped the family fireside for a cramped company of fellow mariners and the occasional harbour bar, lightkeepers had volunteered for a spell in solitary, for a hermitage, for a daily nine-hour discipline of Cistercian silence.

That sense of monastic vocation was confirmed when I climbed floor by floor through each level, each 'cell', of Hook Lighthouse (52.13°N 6.93°W) in County Wexford, the second oldest light in the world, which began as a beacon tended by actual 5th-century monks. The present structure, built prior to 1240, was also built by monks (Cistercians, in fact) with its 12-foot-thick walls, and each floor's chamber rib-vaulted in the manner of Europe's great 12th-century abbeys and cathedrals.

VIGIL

The one remaining lighthouse clockface
breathes its last this November morning.

Black bitumen walls heave a sigh,
continue a tick-tock, tick-tocking,
over the next days' watchfulness
while a gathering Force 10 musters.

The already-leaking roof seeps rain
unrelenting into the Lamp Room,
into the main Oil Storage Room,
inwards, downwards, seawards.

A cowled brotherhood on the seabed
toll matins in unison until solace arrives
in the form of a rowboat, a painted rowboat,
freshly blue, circuiting a deadly undertow,
knifing through jolting waves, a boat on a mission.

The incoming tide disappears without trace.
Landside wives pray,
knowing little can be salvaged.

DOMESTICITY

When lighthouse life was normal, and weather unremarkable, most lighthouse-men simply carried out their timetabled light-keeping duties and a set domestic routine, a routine Jeanette Winterson's *Lighthousekeeping* narrator recounts: sock-washing, tea-making, cooking bacon and chops, and inevitably sluicing the very many stairs. Cooking could, in fact, be a challenge, with limited facilities and weather-dependent supplies. And pastimes, for the off-duty hours, could include anything from lone chess, to building ships in bottles, listening to the wireless, playing fiddle or mouth organ, and reading epic sea tales.

> VLADIMIR: *That passed the time.*
> ESTRAGON: *It would have passed in any case.*
> VLADIMIR: *Yes, but not so rapidly.*
> – Samuel Beckett, *Waiting for Godot*

QUIETLY CRAZY

Humdrum domesticity and regular-as-clockwork duties disguise both the isolation – the sort of thing most of us imagine would drive us mad – and the high seriousness of lighthouse keepers' responsibilities. Glimpsed briefly in a report I saw pinned to the wall at Cape Cod's Highland Lighthouse, in which a 19th-century head keeper had to justify, at length, to the authorities, his light having failed on a particular night.

But it is the loneliness and the drama, not the *light housekeeping*, that stay in the public perception, that fascinate us as they captivated poet Henry Wadsworth Longfellow, whose dramatic invocation, *The Lighthouse*, was inspired by Portland Head Light. Or attracted solitude's great champion, Henry David Thoreau, a frequent visitor to Highland Light (recounting how 80 feet of cliff fell away one night, the building, like Aquinnah Light on Martha's Vineyard, among others, having been rollered back from the brink, time and again, in its history).

ABANDONED

Maybe our puzzling, as we grew up, over what a lighthouse life can do to the soul was fuelled by Wilf Gibson's poem in which *three men alive on Flannan Isle…dwelt on three men dead.*

Not that anyone was sure they were dead, but their quarters were abandoned *á la Mary Celeste.*

Built on Eilean Mór, west of the Outer Hebrides/Western Isles, by David Alan Stevenson, cousin of Robert Louis, Flannan Isles Lighthouse (58.28°N 7.59°W) had its share of problems and dangers, none of which, though, could account for the inexplicable disappearance of the keepers in 1900: for which no credible explanation was forthcoming, then or since. All sorts of theories have, however, been proposed, from supernatural occurrences to *monsters from the deep,* from high winds to a freak tsunami, and even, in some speculations, murder!

The Flannan mystery appeared, in 1900, to become a focus for society's wariness of both nature and the supernatural, for its suspicion of those who choose isolation, and for its emerging obsession with human psychology, our relationship with the sea becoming a mirror, at a moment in time, for all our subconscious fears.

UNMANNED

Much of the mystery has gone now, along with the imposed solitude: 1500 years after that first beacon at Hook was lit, lighthouses on both sides of the Atlantic have been unmanned for more than twenty years.

Heading into the Lighthouse Commissioners' office in Edinburgh, you pass under a model of the Bell Rock Lighthouse (almost a toy, a souvenir, with the innocence of a seaside helter-skelter or a painted lighthouse on a trips-round-the-bay signboard) and enter the calm of the august panelled boardroom, the one with the incredibly island-and-inlet-dotted coastal map that started my quest.

And above that oak-lined grandeur where so many vital decisions were taken, in a control centre one floor up, an array of computer monitors have replaced, in this automated age, all those lonely anchorites, those patient watchers, frying herring in stone cells high above storm-tossed breakers.

THE LIGHTHOUSE STEVENSONS' LIGHTHOUSES

JMW Turner's crashing-seas portrayal of that same Bell Rock Lighthouse (designed as frontispiece for Robert Stevenson's account of its construction on a submerged reef off Arbroath) offers more impressive evidence of Stevenson's engineering achievement, his battle with the elements, than does the little over-door *maquette*.

Bell Rock Lighthouse (56.43°N 2.39°W) is just one of Stevenson's many, including the Barra Head Light, built too late to offer guidance to those McNeil migrants heading for Cape Breton or the Antrim Glens.

His 1817 Corsewall Point Lighthouse has marked many of my Larne-Stranraer migrations (and was a crucial point of reference in the early stages of the MV *Princess Victoria*'s tragic journey) but the Robert Stevenson achievement with which I was more familiar as a child was the Mull of Kintyre Lighthouse which he rebuilt in 1826, having helped his future father-in-law, Thomas Smith, construct the original building in 1788.

An achievement, not least because materials had to be carted by pack-horse the 12 miles from the Firth of Clyde's Campbelltown (55.43°N 5.61°W), the port directly across the North Channel from Cushendall, the port to which a daily ferry ran from our local Red Bay Pier when I was growing up.

And familiar, because the Mull of Kintyre was such a significant point of reference on all I could know, gazing out to sea in Cushendall childhood years, of any *far shore*.

LEGACY

Three of Robert Stevenson's sons, Alan, David and Thomas, became lighthouse engineers themselves, though in the following generation only David's sons took on the mantle of guardians of the deep. Alan's son Bob (Robert Alan Mowbray Stevenson) became an art critic and moved to Chiswick, where I now live in London, and Robert Louis, Thomas's son, would become the famous creator of *Treasure Island*, frequenting Bob's Chiswick literary circles before moving to the Monterey Peninsula opposite Point Lobos in California, and from there to Western Samoa where he lived out his sea-girt island days.

21: Infinitude

THE LAST LIGHTHOUSE KEEPER

Another nine-hour watch. One good lens locked
on a lowlands horizon, a smoky night. In a paraffin
fugue he's moonstruck, brow on his numbed forearm.
An untethered mind can measure subliminal static.
A compulsive tap-tapping from fathoms below,
due north-north-east where dry land is submerged
memory, where spires & gables accrete like coral
in the standstill of underwater aeons,
where unmirrored parlours crawl with hermit crabs.

Bell hours never toll in these unmarked resting places.
A former mariner shoulders his way along the sea's
corridors, pocket-compass needle quivering on south
for an infinitude of nautical miles, a false spiral
of airbubbles trailing from his halibut mouth.
Voices of the already drowned cannot drown a second time.
The submerged clutch at parched memories of that stark
final thirst. *Some dream the clanking anchor, the judder
of landfall.* Soon it is dawn light over Vatersay.
The keeper shrugs his mind into hesitant life, logs
calculations in the chillest hour.

Only the flittering singeing of spider-lamp moths
for company. He packs telescope, his half-hunter,
sidereal charts, descends the cast-iron barnacled spiral.
On Watchman's Row a cold, cold hearth is set, awaits
a struck match. *Loneliness & a rocky bed lurk for us all,
now & at the hour.* Nothing above the solitary watcher
but the great curvature, the unbearable sweetness
of earth's gravity.

22: Boatman

The waves were steeped deep-blue
save for a pattern of diamond-pointed light on their backs
which rippled as the backs of great horses
ripple with muscles as they move.
The waves fell; withdrew and fell again…
– Virginia Woolf, *The Waves*

ATTAINING THE UNATTAINABLE

Virginia Woolf recognised that lighthouses speak to us of both individual isolation and ultimate interdependence.

But there's a deeper explanation for her writing a whole novel about wanting to make it 'to the lighthouse', about that hankering that anyone will know who has watched, fascinated, those cliff and rock-based guardians, as Virginia did from Talland House, her family's holiday home, high above St Ives Bay, gazing north-east to Godrevy Lighthouse (50.24°N 5.40°W). A gaze to which she would return, firstly as a teenager with the family after her mother's death, later as a young woman lodging at the nearby Badger Inn, and again, years later, staying at the Carbis Bay Hotel with her husband, Leonard, in the 1930s.

Woolf's fifth novel, *To the Lighthouse*, published in 1928 with an iconic 'lighthouse' cover-design by her sister Vanessa Bell, focuses not so much on the promised adventure itself but on the Ramsay family (fictionalised versions of her own parents and siblings), on inner emotional turmoil, on expectation, longing, disappointment, loss, and time's passing.

McALISTERS

I've never been sure whether I owe my fondness for the novel to shared lighthouse longings or to Virginia's choosing to place the action, not in Cornwall where her family actually holidayed, but on the Isle of Skye, directly north of Cushendall (though like Melville, who hadn't visited Nantucket when he wrote *Moby Dick*, Woolf didn't visit Skye until a decade after the novel was published).

The other connection to my coastal world is that the local fishermen who take the Ramsay family out to the lighthouse were called McAlister, as were some of the fishing families we knew in Cushendall, due south of Skye.

To the Lighthouse is continually on edge with the possibility of failure inherent in any such promised expedition: a disappointment that I once experienced on setting out with some friends, McAlisters included, in our teenage years, to cross from Cushendall to Rathlin Island, beyond Torr Head and directly opposite Robinson Jeffers's beloved Fair Head; Marconi's Rathlin; Rathlin of the three lighthouses, which fact alone should have told us these were treacherous waters.

Predictably, before we'd reached Torr Head, the Moyle betrayed us and we were forced to sail for home, though even rounding Layde looked impossible and we considered landfall at Cushendun. Home safe in the end, and strangely wiser.

ABSENCE AND LONGING

But something more than disappointment lies at the emotional heart of Woolf's novel. A central theme, inevitably as time passes between early and later family holidays, is the absence of Mrs Ramsay, an absence that reflects Virginia's own loss, at age thirteen, and, one guesses, her sense (a sense I share) that going back to a coastal place of optimism and seemingly endless summers can never be an unmixed pleasure.

If Camilla, in the novel, conveys Virginia's teenage longing for an earlier time when her mother was present, the act of exploring those feelings through *To the Lighthouse* when she was in her forties conveys something more. Woolf would return to St Ives Bay time and again as an adult, to gaze at unattainable Godrevy Lighthouse, as I've done on this quest, from the garden of Talland House: that gazing tells me less about sentinels and horizons, and much more about daughters and mothers, about loss and irretrievability. And about those conflicting meanings Woolf attributed to lighthouses: our mutual dependence and our ultimate isolation.

23: Still Farther North

I've always had a day dream of being a light-house keeper, absolutely alone…a wonderful cold rocky shore in the Falklands, or a house in Nova Scotia on the bay, <u>exactly</u> like my grandmother's…
Perhaps it is a recurrent need.
– Elizabeth Bishop, letter to Robert Lowell

TRUE NORTH, AGAIN, MAPLESS

Journeying mapless and destinationless: but not simply messing about in boats, on scenic coastal drives, on bridges, causeways, piers and headlands. Not merely seeing, but seeking, *en route*, to understand how, perhaps, we'd been out of our depths as a family when my mother became ill, how my coastal memories, slipway games, fishing gear, my ships on the horizon, would always be interwoven with thoughts of her, as a newly wed in the third-last house from the point with the sea's exultations on three sides, and then as someone cast adrift for a time after my father's sudden illness.

Not solely the recklessness of going beyond the breakwater and buffeting the metaphorical waves, like 'inlander' Emily Dickinson.

Not just sandpiper restlessness, like Elizabeth Bishop's love of, obsession with, shorelines.

Not just the unrequited destination like Virginia Woolf's *Lighthouse*.

Not solely the longing for a happier family time, the yearning for lost completeness.

The clue was 'north': not 'finding North' in some abstract sense. But 'going north'.

Going south annually (in the family Hillman whose glove compartment I've described as being full of rumpled, unusable maps) always meant sunshine, human warmth, gregariousness, ease. *La dolce vita*. The opposite of north. And yet it seemed to me that actually finding Melville's *true places*, the places that might explain something to me, meant going further north. While 'farther' refers to physical distance and 'further' is used for abstract, metaphorical distance, both are equally significant in this stretch of the exploration.

NORTH OF NEW ENGLAND

I'd always thought I understood Bostonian Elizabeth Bishop's desire for the sea, her longing for that horizon gaze. And I'd long had a vague idea that the North Haven she'd written about was North Haven in Connecticut, south of Boston, near East Haven, West Haven and New Haven, all on Long Island Sound, a stone's throw from the Hamptons and New York.

So that Sunday spent with Kate Quinn on Bishop's actual North Haven Island in Maine was a revelation. A world away from her friend Lowell's nearby summer home at Castine, even, a pristine white-clapboard village that attracted New York literati and Bostonian wealth (*summer millionaires* in Lowell's *Skunk Hour* poem).

Underpopulated, and remote, North Haven living seemed closer to life on my Antrim coast, which Bishop had once visited.

CROSSING BORDERS

To find my 'True North' then, I knew I'd have to travel to the Canadian border, beyond Lubec. Though one could have delayed indefinitely at that sleepy town, its name and architecture borrowed from the Hanseatic port of Lübeck (if replicated in white clapboard), and with its iconic candy-striped West Quoddy Light beaming lightwaves round the earth's curvature to Africa: 3,000 miles away, admittedly, but still the nearest point in the US to the Atlantic's far shore.

Lunenburg, in predominantly French/Scottish Canada proved even more Germanic than Lubec, with its black-&-white carpenter-Gothic spires, its fairytale 18th-century rainbow-coloured wooden homes, warehouses, and harbour bars, a bustling many-masted port, and its own 'Lunenburg Dutch', a blend of German and US English: unsurprising, given that, up to the 1950s, half the population had German ethnic background.

Though all that was yet to come, farther north, after Belfast, Maine (with its small shipbuilding industry), after Bangor, Maine, and the Penobscot Nation's Indian Island. On past New Brunswick. Past the border array of saltires between Aulac and Fort Lawrence proclaiming Nova Scotia's Scottish roots.

And finally, on the edge of darkness, through the Cobequid Pass toll station (where I hadn't brought any Canadian dollars and left with an IOU as they don't take credit cards after hours). And on down to Cobequid Bay's Great Village, where I would live, briefly, in the house in which Elizabeth Bishop did her growing up.

GREAT VILLAGE HOME

Cape Breton was still ahead, still farther north, and days to go.

Only that far north would I grasp how someone like Elizabeth's mother, Gertrude Bulmer, from as far north already as Great Village NS, could become so homesick simply by moving to a more northerly part of Nova Scotia. I had yet to learn that, when Gertrude went there as a trainee teacher, Cape Breton was still an island, accessible only by ferry crossing, and not long settled by some 50,000 Gaelic-speaking Scots fleeing a century of Highland Clearances (the Bulmers being of predominantly English heritage).

Whether Gertrude had felt less homesick later when she went south to Boston, to stay with her sisters, I don't know. Though she was soon to be back in Great Village as her Bostonian husband, William, died when their daughter Elizabeth was just eight months old. And soon after that, following a breakdown, she was to disappear completely from her daughter's life.

MOUNT CARMEL SUNDAY

A cry runs the transverse length
of the buildings. Clean, uncreasing
like a man's handkerchief. The line
of short-stay cabins jolts. Haven
of the isolated, internalised, the bereft.
Family saloons arrive with ginger cordial,
cartons of clotted-cream fudge.
This cry
stalls over Reserved Parking
invades pink kimonos, scalloped matinee
jackets, blackout blinds, pillowcases
stacked on drystore shelves; it billows over
elm, yew & rowan, cleaves awkward
but sure to the weatherboard spire
of a neighbouring hawthorned province.

from Understudies

VISITING, AND NOT VISITING

I had found much to love in Great Village: the bay, the old graveyard, the firehouse, the ESSO filling station, the last of these reminiscent of Bishop's poem celebrating family love in what some might think an unlikely setting, a message reinforced by her optimistic ending line, *Somebody loves us all,* and made all the more poignant by the homely touches, around the functional workplace, of a mother who never appears in the poem.

But it was the Great Village Post Office with its *Canada Post/Postes Canada* sign that really brought me home: the virtually unchanged post office to which, every week, Elizabeth took a quarter and a parcel, packed by her grandmother and addressed in indelible purple to her mother in the Mount Hope Asylum in Dartmouth, an address she would try awkwardly to conceal from neighbours on the way.

Not that I had to post parcels to my mother in the periods during which she was being treated in Holywell Hospital, 30 miles away from home, but I did experience an awkwardness with adults who – in a village community that otherwise so supports families – didn't know what to say to a child about her mother's mental breakdown.

Strange to ponder, days later, after Great Village, and looking out over Dartmouth Cove (44.67°N 63.57°W) following a reading at Dartmouth's Alderney Gate Library which included poems about my mother and talk of Elizabeth Bishop... Strange to find myself in Mount Hope's car park looking up to the red-brick walls and institutional windows that Bishop never saw while her mother was a patient there for nearly twenty years.

And strange to remember my own teenage Sunday afternoons in Holywell's car park, a place I have found it paradoxically comforting to revisit occasionally over the many years since my mother's time there.

PILGRIMAGE

Like it's a re-run of the Sunday visits,
but once a year, late evening, summer usually.
Perennially unchanged.
                     Tall pines,
'Fifties asbestos roofing on 'The Villa',
the green-varnished verandah chair that's
never used. Silence broken only by rooks.

The tower clock's shown 1.30 for nineteen years.
There's always a lone post-war ambulance
parked up at 'Rosgrove', awaiting the call.

from *House of Small Absences*

MOUNT HOPE

As a name, *Mount Hope* seems ironic, especially in the context of someone being detained there without hope of release for 18 years.

I had found a strange completeness in the fact that my mother started her married life in a house called *Glendun* and ended her days, after cancer treatment, in a nursing home also called *Glendun*. It seems somehow sadly apt, then, that Elizabeth Bishop – never having had a chance to visit her mother at *Mount Hope* in Dartmouth – should have been laid to rest finally in a place called 'hope', *Hope Cemetery* in Worcester, Massachusetts.

THE SCREAM

It can't simply have been the 70 miles from Great Village to Dartmouth that prevented Elizabeth seeing her mother, as she was twenty-three and a Vassar graduate by the time her mother died in 1934. Raised firstly by her mother's parents in Great Village, she was subsequently looked after by the Boston side of the family, though with frequent visits back to Nova Scotia. Clearly both sides of the family thought Elizabeth should not be in contact with her mother.

Maybe the equivalent of my 'pilgrimages' to Holywell weren't possible for Bishop, as there had been no recovery, no 'after', in her mother's case. Every breakdown, has its own trajectory, its own degree of severity – my mother's after my father's illness, Elizabeth Bishop's mother's, after her husband's early death.

A scream, the echo of a scream,
hangs over that Nova Scotian village.
No one hears it.
– Elizabeth Bishop, *In the Village*

What we do know from Bishop's writing is that their final separation followed an anguished scream from her mother: and Elizabeth's bedroom, where I spent some time, the room next to the one in which her mother screamed, was, for me, one of the *true places* that aren't on any map.

The 'scream' moment involved a dress-fitting with local dress-maker, Miss O'Neill, and with Elizabeth's grandmother and aunts – the mother and sisters that Gertrude had come 'home' to live with after William's death – all involved in the consultation: a moment that has taken on a dream-like tableau quality for me, with roles played by my mother, her grandmother and those McNeill dressmaker aunts, all years younger than when I knew them.

THE BACK PORCH

The room, the scream, the village post office and Mount Hope asylum, are all, I realise, part of understanding Elizabeth Bishop. Her sandpiper quality, her choosing North Haven, or Breton Cove, or the Antrim Coast, her writing about islands, her titling her first poetry collection *Geography* and her discovering – and living in – Ouro Preto in Brazil, all speak of a restlessness, a need for coasts, for the sea.

In a private poem written in Brazil and unpublished in her lifetime Bishop wrote, *my compass / still points north / to wooden houses*. According to her friend, and owner of the Ouro Preto house, Dona Linda Nemer, Bishop did, in fact, travel with a compass and slept with her head aligned to north, though the poem is really yearning, not merely for magnetic north but, despite the attractions of the southern hemisphere, for Boston Bay, North Haven, Great Village and beyond.

The lodestone power of north for Bishop is perhaps best understood by sitting on the back porch of her grandparents' wooden house looking across Cobequid Bay towards Burnt-coat Lighthouse. Or perhaps on the front porch of weatherboarded Sabine Farmhouse on North Maine's North Haven Island, looking across Penobscot Bay to Rockland Breakwater Lighthouse.

Or north of McNeil Beach Lighthouse, at the clapboard house in Breton Cove (46.46°N 60.46°W, finally encountered on the latter stages of the US/Canada section of my journey) where Bishop spent six weeks in 1947, looking out over St Ann's Bay to Ciboux Island, or Neil's Harbour, or Point Aconi.

THAT SAME SEA

All three of Bishop's lighthouses stand guard over the same North Atlantic ocean that Virginia Woolf could see beyond Godrevy Light; that lay behind the Rathlin lighthouses I failed to reach on an impulsive boat trip; that crashed on winter nights below the Mull of Kintyre lighthouse I watched from Cushendall; that same sea that lapped rocky Limerick Point below my childhood home.

SOMETIMES I FEEL LIKE…

And in Breton Cove, and North Haven, I thought again about the part played in Bishop's adult life, in her development, in her restlessness, by her 'orphan' upbringing in the care of Bulmer grandparents and Bishop aunts and uncles, like so many children in an age of high parental mortality.

Cause and effect relationships aren't, though, clear-cut. Lucy Maud Montgomery, for example, was brought up by her Macneill grandparents, on Scottish Catholic-and-Presbyterian-settled Prince Edward Island, next to Cape Breton in Canada's Maritimes. Her mother had died and her father moved to Saskatchewan. She taught on PEI after leaving university in

Halifax, and turned her childhood, and her teenage experience of her cousin David Macneill's 'Green Gables' farmhouse, into an uplifting and popular story of overcoming adversity, quite untypical of, say, Woolf's or Bishop's responses to loss.

Like Montgomery, my mother had been brought up by McNeill grandparents, in her case between the Catholic Glens and Presbyterian Clough, child of a seldom-mentioned Catholic-Protestant mixed marriage.

My grandmother, Mary McNeill, living in East Belfast with her shipyard-worker husband, William Reilly, fell victim to the post-Great-War influenza pandemic (that same 'flu whose victims Bishop's Bulmer aunts nursed in Boston). Her sister Jane died but Mary recovered for several years only to fall seriously ill again with repercussions from the viral damage in the year before my mother was born.

So my mother (Mary Jane Reilly, named after her mother and her mother's dead sister) was brought up by her maternal grandparents in Glenravel, away from parents and siblings, with her mother finally dying when she was seven. Her father died of cancer when she was eleven, and both those loved McNeill grandparents passed on soon after.

NO HORIZONS

How fragile is life for a motherless girl? How much can her own mother's absence during my mother's childhood explain what happened to her, to our family, in my teenage years? How much do parallel absences in Bishop's childhood, in Woolf's teenage years, explain their adult lives? Or the deep psychological empathy in their writing?

Unlike Gertrude Bishop, my mother would find stability again, and decades later, on daily Coast Road drives during her final short illness, we found time to watch the horizon and talk together of our family's troubled years, and of her own motherless childhood. Shared memories and conversations that only add to my need, since, to spend time on those same shorelines, gazing.

What I do know at the end of my searching is that some of us who return endlessly to the edges of oceans don't do so simply to recapture a lost past before family life was, in some sense, set adrift for a time.

Our need is clearly to find a place (Bishop at Breton Cove, or North Haven, or Cobequid Bay, Woolf at St Ives and Carbis Bay, say) where we can look out beyond distractions, past busy boatyards, fishing ports, breakwaters and harbour walls. Past so much that defines the limits of the familiar.

Where we can gaze on a distant horizon that we know is imaginary anyway, a geometric and geographical construct, an optical illusion, and recognise that we are, some of us, endlessly, and not discontentedly, all at sea, with no promise of, no need for, the solace of a *far shore*.

I feel I can say, at last, with Lily Briscoe at the end of Woolf's *To the Lighthouse,* that *I have had my vision.*

24: Soundscape

CHARTING THE UNKNOWN

Charting inshore waters already meant 'home' to me but it was the thin map-line between familiar and unknown that I needed to trace, rather than the deep sea of Odysseus' epic voyages, Melville's titanic struggles, the heart of Conrad's dark interior, the delirium of Coleridge's *hot and copper* ocean skies.

And what I found, in seaports, coves, headlands, bays – and in books – is that whether settings-out from shore fulfil dreams or end in simple disappointment or full-blown maritime tragedy, nothing can stop us sandpipers being pulled back to coasts and islands.

Nothing can stop our gazing out from piers and promontories, lookouts and lighthouses, holiday homes and scenic view-points, not because we believe, necessarily, that a far shore even exists, but because longing itself is, for us, a constant.

Chance, perhaps, that the seascapes and life-stories of some of my loved writers, Virginia Woolf and Elizabeth Bishop especially, map very closely to my own, or my mother's, but through those lives and writings I've found, in some senses, a sea-chart with which to navigate the past, and an understanding that looking out from shore isn't simply an expression of longing for a lost time.

The search started with no printed map: and ends in a visual and aural coast-scape brought to tentative, liminal realisation in broken soundwaves, lighthouse signals, submerged voices, cliff paths, Morse messages, distress calls, static, forgotten island songs, car headlights, stars, a gate's creak – in the familiar chaos of half-remembered dreams.

NIGHT MUSIC

Late last, lone crossing
out of a redundant
Stranraer ferry port
millpond night, security gate

Maidens Lights far out
high-speed car-beams scythe on each
inward/outward bend, main streets

inns, harbours, fish-farms,
sea-walls, Monterey cypress
all along the coast flash past,
bay by bay, head by head
(Maine's chain of piers & harbours,
the long road from Crookhaven
to Hook & back)

longwave Home Service
Ballachulish or Girvan transmitter

Vln 1

I saw the   Har - bour Lights,   they on - ly told   me you   were   part - ing.

postwar dance-band programme
static fuzz, crackle, echoes

rattle of Singer bobbin, treadle whirr
in the good front room overlooking
Limerick Point
…last Coast Road arch
passed, Red Bay Pier ferry
you slow, brake, park

shivering light
through branches at Newe's

stop, one deep breath,
cross to Hannah's shop door,
shudder, think
school icy morning huddle

phone-box, insistent ringing
don't answer
-. --- / ..-. .- .-. / ... . --- .-. .

124

-. --- / ..-. .- .-. / ... . --- .-. .

school-bus revs at the bend
you walk past the flattened crop-circle
of a departed circus-field circus:

> *bluish black-&-white TV flicker*
> *through kitchen door*

cold-store out back
where you fetched extra Tuesday buttermilk

> *next-bungalow*
> *front-doorstep melodeon-player*
> *(Elizabeth playing parlor-organ*
> *Newfoundland lodging house, 1932)*

-. --- / ..-. .- .-. / ... . --- .-. .

round by Danny M's increasingly precise
high box-hedge

> *click-clack of improbably late shears*
> *in last of pre-midnight*
> *street-lighting*

no-left-turn, not a night for direct
route home, take it slow
after all this time

> *one of your mother's songs*
> *— one of her mother's —*
> *from the Divis mast & through*
> *a latched-open kitchen window,*
> *a neighbour's*

Sing me a song of a lad that is gone, Say could that lad be I?

long way round
railway carriage, verandah-house,
jewel in the plantation,
lush, unfamiliar date palms
giant *Little Prince* baobabs

> *town siren calling up*
> *Achill coastguard, Rockland lifeboat,*
> *Great Village Volunteer Fire Brigade*

slatted willow-pattern bridge
to a stone-cold beach shelter seat
below the Portofino-white house
distant bluebell sward
Salmon Port fishing-hut slatted bench
(Nantucket's Brant Point
or down at Breton Cove
same square clouded window bolted
against night ocean)

> *Marconi Beach signal*
> *past Rathlin, Fair Head,*
> *straight to Cornwall*
> *the president via Morse*
> *– ingenuity…perfecting a system…*
> *wireless telegraphy…cordial –*
> *lost in static, crackle*
> -. --- / ..-. .- .-. / ... . --- .-. .

skylight latched shut
on Cobequid Bay,
child waiting for stars, raindrops:
Great Village house
father long-gone, troubled
grandparents' conversation about Gertrude

> *dial hovering*
> *on Light Programme*
> *East Belfast Flute Band*
> *'Nearer my God to Thee'*
> *played at march tempo*
> *for all the shipyard workers lost*

a young Marconi
in his father's mansion
tuning in to

> *last strains of the ship's*
> *augmented final-night orchestra*
> *years in the future*
> -. --- / ..-. .- .-. / ... . --- .-.

someone, perhaps my mother
rounding the point on foot

watches search-beamed
January night, north

three hundred & seventy
McNeils pass unlighted
Barra Head, unmanned
Flannan, bound for
St Ann's Bay, a lake of gold

scanning south
dead search goes on

as Rose McNeill (14) leaves
Clarendon Dock, Belfast (1911)
stands with liner-rail crowds
along Saint Lawrence River
nine days later

-. --- / ..-. .- .-. / ... . --- .-. .

safe passage, generations
of packed migrant ships,
letters from America, dots & dashes
dispersed
shipping, sound
or sinking throughout icy waters

intermittent flash
the Mull, Barra, Cape Wrath,
echo up & down
hazardous Maine &
Maritimes coastline
-. --- / ..-. .- .-. / ... . --- .-. .

you creep through
glossy laurel undergrowth
then her hydrangea bushes
either side of the gate
– *bluest for miles around* –
from the regular
iron filing scoopfuls
brought home from his garage

radiogram inside
no one hears
salt-rusted hinge
creak

needing a touch of
his 3-in-One Oil (!)
gloss-painted front door

& tap-tap on
frosted glass panel
no answer

perennial wallflowers

side-path gravel crunches

past parsley & shallots

lolly sticks propping up
colour-burst seed-packets
from Stephenson
Brothers, Shore Street
-. --- / ..-. .- .-. / ... . --- .-. .

catch gable-wall
pebbledash brush against
your sleeve, gable-end
that weathered a lifetime's
East Wind buffeting
November to February
yearly, canopied monkey-puzzle
giving cover, a touch
of exotic as ever

radiogram static fading out
-. --- / ..-. .- .-. / ... . --- .-. .

128

and the waves, the rising seas
tang the air
with old saltwater sweetness

the kitchen door opens
& voices rise

what took you so long,
we've been here all day.

Acknowledgements

While my interest in coastal lives owes a great deal to family, friends, neighbours in the Antrim Glens, and to people in so many sea's-edge locations I've visited over the years including those I've experienced specifically as a writer, an Arts Council England Grants for the Arts award has been of particular importance in facilitating my travel and writing over an eighteen-month period.

My engagement with each location was hosted by a range of individuals, organisations, venues and writers' groups who hosted my *Edge of the Depths* writing workshops and *Voyage Out* words-and-music performances. Individuals too numerous to list, but thanks to all of you. Organisations/venues included Ulster University International Literary Festival (Coleraine), Poetry in Aldeburgh (Suffolk), Ballyeamon Barn & Cushendall Golf Club (County Antrim), Crickhowell Literary Festival (Powys), Suffolk Poetry Society, Poetry Salon (Boston MA), Pathways Arts (Martha's Vineyard MA), PWGM Writers' Social Group (Portland ME), Merrill Memorial Library (Falmouth ME), Bangor Public Library (Bangor ME), Evergreen Writers (Halifax NS), Alderney Gate Library (Dartmouth NS), Lunenburg School of the Arts (Lunenburg NS), Charles Causley Festival (Launceston, Cornwall), George Mackay Brown Fellowship & Stromness Library (Orkney), Assynt Crofters Trust (Sutherland), forWords (Forres Writing Group) & Findhorn Village Centre (Moray), North Uist Writers & Taigh Chearsabhagh Museum & Arts Centre (Lochmaddy, North Uist), O Bhéal (Cork), Hooked on Poetry (Duncannon, County Wexford), Dylan Thomas Centre (Swansea), Torbay Festival of Poetry, and Coffee-House Poetry at the Troubadour (London).

Thanks, too, to those who hosted my earlier coastal/island residencies including Tor House Foundation (Carmel CA), South Beach Lookout (Aldeburgh, Suffolk) and Heinrich Böll

Cottage, (Achill Island, County Mayo). And thanks to Lenoir-Rhyne University (Hickory, North Carolina) for a Visiting Writers Series residency in which I completed this manuscript.

Special thanks are due to Kate Quinn of North Haven Library who proved a welcoming and informative guide to Elizabeth Bishop's island holiday home (14: *Island Notes*), and to the Elizabeth Bishop Society of Nova Scotia and St. James Church of Great Village Preservation Society, who enabled me to stay for a time in the Bishop-Bulmer House in Great Village NS, both experiences proving real inspirations on this coastal quest.

Sources

Elizabeth Bishop's thoughts on aloneness (in 8: *Chasing Sand-pipers*) are from a 1929 essay in Walnut Hill School magazine *The Blue Pencil* quoted in Brett C. Miller, *Elizabeth Bishop: Life and the Memory of It* (University of California), and her light-house longings, from a letter to Robert Lowell (in 23: *Still Farther North*), are to be found in *Words in Air*, ed. Thomas Travisano & Saskia Hamilton (Faber). Her story *In the Village* appeared in *The New Yorker* in December 1953 and poem quotations are from *Elizabeth Bishop: Complete Poems* (Chatto) except for the lines quoted in 'THE BACK PORCH' (in 23: *Still Farther North*) from the posthumously published poem begin-ning 'Dear, my compass / still points north' which appears in *Edgar Allen Poe & The Juke Box: Uncollected Poems, Drafts and Fragments* (ed. Alice Quinn, Farrar Strauss & Giroux).

Excerpts from novels, songs and a play are attributed within the text: other poems, from which lines are quoted, 'Le cimi-tière marin' by Paul Valéry, 'The Harbour in the Evening' by Tom Paulin, 'Sea Surface Full of Clouds' by Wallace Stevens, and 'Voyages' by Hart Crane, are taken from their respective collections, *Charmes* (Folio), *The Strange Museum* (Faber), *The Collected Poems of Wallace Stevens* (Vintage), and *The Complete Poems and Selected Letters and Prose of Hart Crane* (Liveright).

The poems 'No Far Shore' and 'Mount Carmel Sunday' are taken from my *Understudies: New and Selected Poems* (Seren): 'Pilgrimage' is from my latest collection *House of Small Absences* (Seren).

Stories of RMS *Titanic* and MV *Princess Victoria* have come to me through family and local conversations as well as a wide variety of published sources, one of the most informative regarding the latter tragedy being *Death in the North Channel: the Loss of the Princess Victoria* by Stephen Cameron (Colour-point Books).